REA's Bo
They have resc

(a sample of the <u>hundreds of letters</u> REA receives each year)

(more on next page)

(continued from previous page)

"Your books have saved my GPA, and quite possibly my sanity. My course grade is now an 'A', and I couldn't be happier."

Student, Winchester, IN

"These books are the best review books on the market. They are fantastic!"

Student, New Orleans, LA

"Your book was responsible for my success on the exam. . . I will look for REA the next time I need help."

Student, Chesterfield, MO

"I think it is the greatest study guide I have ever used!"

Student, Anchorage, AK

"I encourage others to buy REA because of their superiority. Please continue to produce the best quality books on the market."

Student, San Jose, CA

"Just a short note to say thanks for the great support your book gave me in helping me pass the test . . . I'm on my way to a B.S. degree because of you !"

Student, Orlando, FL

Super Review™

All You Need to Know!

BASIC MUSIC

By the Staff of
Research & Education Association
Dr. M. Fogiel, Director
Carl Fuchs, Chief Editor

Based on Music Courses & Teaching Materials
of the U.S. Government

Research & Education Association
61 Ethel Road West
Piscataway, New Jersey 08854

SUPER REVIEW™
OF BASIC MUSIC

Printed in the United States of America

Library of Congress Control Number 2001089902

International Standard Book Number 0-87891-385-8

SUPER REVIEW is a trademark of
Research & Education Association, Piscataway, New Jersey 08854

WHAT THIS Super Review WILL DO FOR YOU

This **Super Review** provides all that you need to know to do your homework effectively and succeed on exams and quizzes.

The book focuses on the core aspects of the subject, and helps you to grasp the important elements quickly and easily.

Outstanding **Super Review** features:

- Based on U.S. Government teaching materials

- Topics are covered in logical sequence

- Topics are reviewed in a concise and comprehensive manner

- The material is presented in student-friendly form that makes it easy to follow and understand

- Individual topics can be easily located

- Provides excellent preparation for midterms, finals and in-between quizzes

- Written by professionals and experts who function as your very own tutors

- Designed for self-study as well as class instruction

- The topics in music are taught without assuming previous familiarity with the subject

- Includes an illustrated dictionary of musical instruments, and a glossary of terms

Dr. Max Fogiel, Director
Carl Fuchs, Chief Editor

CONTENTS

Franz Joseph Haydn

Nature of Sound

Chapter 1

Vibrations

Sound is produced by *vibrations*; there is no sound without *vibrations.* Any musical instrument or other device which produces "sound" vibrates in such a way as to set the surrounding air in vibration. The air in turn becomes a medium of transmission through which these vibrations are carried to the ear.

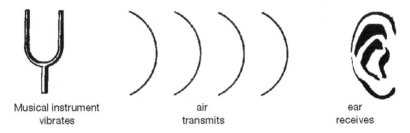

Musical instrument   air   ear
vibrates   transmits   receives

The ear responds by vibrating in sympathy with the incoming vibrations.

Nerve endings in the ear, when stimulated by vibrations, carry this stimulus to the brain, It is in the brain, the final link in the chain, that the result is interpreted as sound.

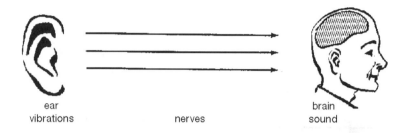

ear
vibrations   nerves   brain
                                    sound

Characteristics of a Musical Tone

Since we recognize sound as anything we can hear, it is necessary to understand the difference between the kinds of sounds. We can immediately identify those sounds which are musical tones and those which are mere noise. Since sound is, as we said, vibrations, let us look at these vibrations a little more closely.

1. Pitch. When the frequency of vibration is regular or even, the sound has *pitch*, and the result is a recognizable musical tone. But when the frequency of vibration is irregular

or uneven there is no recognizable musical tone. We find that a regular "vibration at the frequency of 440 cycles," or, in other words, a speed of 440 even vibrations per second, will produce the pitch "a." An increase in frequency produces a raise in pitch. Any frequency greater than 440 would produce a pitch higher than "a." Conversely, any frequency less than 440 would produce a pitch lower than "a."

2. Intensity. We also find that the more energetic the vibration the louder the sound, or to put it another way, the

greater the *intensity*. Intensity depends on the amplitude of the vibrations.

3. Duration. The length of time a musical tone sounds is called its *duration*.

4. Timbre or Quality. Different kinds of instruments produce different kinds of sounds. A clarinet does not sound like a trombone and *vice versa,* even though they can produce sounds which are identical in pitch, intensity, and duration. This difference is heard as a difference in *tone quality* or *timbre* (pronounced tiamber).

A number of things effect the timbre of musical instruments, among them the fact that some are blown, some are bowed, and still others are plucked or hammered. Timbre is also influenced by the condition of the instrument and the characteristics of individual performers. However, the most fundamental factor influencing timbre is the physical nature of the instrument and the manner in which it vibrates.

Overtones

An investigation of vibrating bodies or generators reveals several important facts:

(1) When set in vibration, a string or air column tends not only to vibrate as one complete unit but also in halves, thirds, fourths, fifths, and so on at the same time.

A Vibrating String

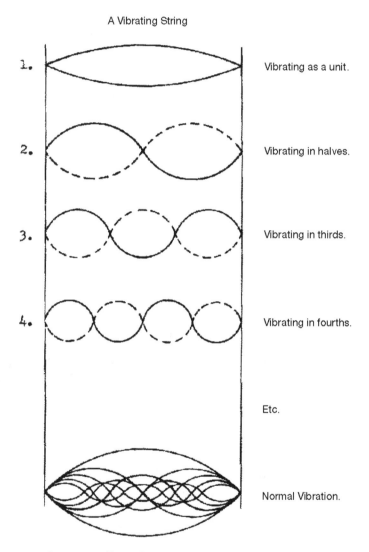

1.   Vibrating as a unit.

2.   Vibrating in halves.

3.   Vibrating in thirds.

4.   Vibrating in fourths.

Etc.

Normal Vibration.

(2) These smaller vibrating parts produce a series of tones called *overtones* (also called *harmonics* or *partials*).

The Overtone Series

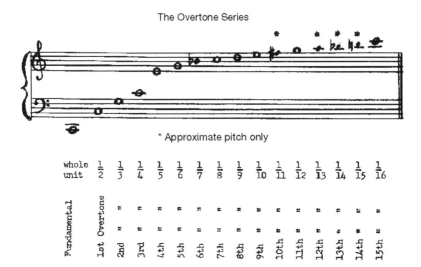

* Approximate pitch only

| whole unit | $\frac{1}{2}$ | $\frac{1}{3}$ | $\frac{1}{4}$ | $\frac{1}{5}$ | $\frac{1}{6}$ | $\frac{1}{7}$ | $\frac{1}{8}$ | $\frac{1}{9}$ | $\frac{1}{10}$ | $\frac{1}{11}$ | $\frac{1}{12}$ | $\frac{1}{13}$ | $\frac{1}{14}$ | $\frac{1}{15}$ | $\frac{1}{16}$ |

(3) The nature of the generator determines how many of these overtones will be audible and to what degree. It is the relative prominence of these overtones which determines the particular timbre we associate with a given instrument. Overtones are usually heard not as individual pitches but as variations in the tone quality of the fundamental.

Prominence of overtones in the flute and clarinet

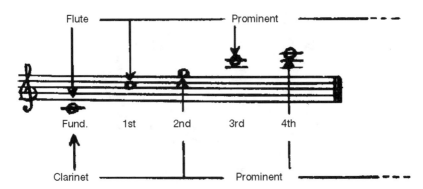

Mendelssohn in his twelfth year

Mendelssohn's Birthplace

Fundamental Notation

The system of notation in common use today is the result of centuries of invention and experimentation. Furthermore, there is no reason to suppose that even now we have reached more than a temporary objective in our search for the ideal tool of communication between composer and performer.

There is a certain group of fundamental symbols now in use which make up the basis of our present-day system, a thorough knowledge of which is essential to the performer and student alike.

Notation of Pitch

The fundamental symbols employed in the representation of pitch are the *Staff, Clefs, Notes,* and *Accidentals.*

The five lines on which the other pitch symbols are notated are called the *Staff.* The lines and spaces of the staff are given alphabetical letter names from A to G inclusive, like the names of the pitches they represent.

Although five lines and four spaces are adequate for one voice or instrument, the combined compass of many voices or instruments includes more pitches than this staff can represent. It is necessary then to provide a staff on which such representation is possible. The staff used for this purpose has eleven lines and ten spaces and is known as the *Great Staff.*

THE GREAT STAFF

'MIDDLE C'

A five-line staff in reality then simply amounts to some part of the great staff. Which part these five lines represent is determined by means of a *clef.* A clef is one of the seven letters placed on one of the lines of the staff thereby assigning a definite pitch to that line.

When it becomes necessary to extend the staff to include pitches above or below, we add *leger* lines:

There are three clefs: the C clef, the G clef, and the F clef. With the passage of time certain decorations as well as simplifications have altered the appearance of the clefs until today,

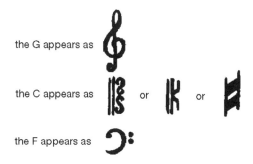

the G appears as

the C appears as

the F appears as

The three clefs in relation to the great staff:

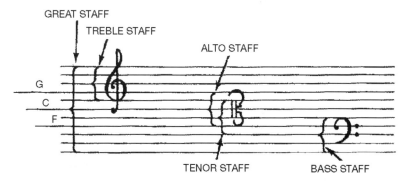

The five-line staves then, can be recognized as some part of the great staff:

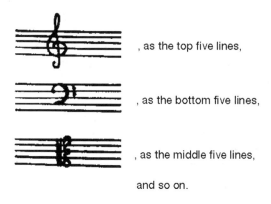

, as the top five lines,

, as the bottom five lines,

, as the middle five lines,

and so on.

With clefs, any five-line portion of the great staff may be identified and used. For instrumental purposes however, only four uses are now common.

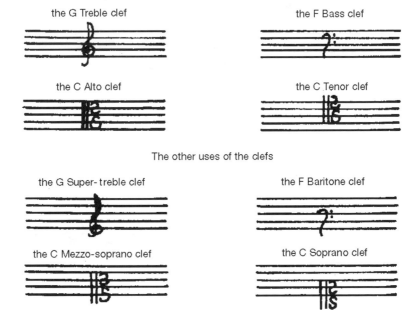

The four common uses of the clefs

the G Treble clef

the F Bass clef

the C Alto clef

the C Tenor clef

The other uses of the clefs

the G Super-treble clef

the F Baritone clef

the C Mezzo-soprano clef

the C Soprano clef

The clef names reflect the early practice of assigning to each voice an appropriate clef.

The staff and clefs having provided the background or framework, the symbols representing specific pitches, called *notes*, are then placed with the notehead on the appropriate line or space:

f   g   a   b   etc.

Those pitches which occur "between" the letter names and are not representable by lines and spaces alone require additional symbols for proper identification. These symbols, known as *accidentals*, are five in number and will be discussed fully in chapters 4 and 5.

Notation of Duration

Duration of tone as represented by any symbol is determined by the speed at which the music is played; the relative duration is represented by the shape or position of the symbol itself. If we consider duration in terms of regularly occurring pulses or "beats," four of which would be equal to the symbol O or *whole note*, a table of relative values can be established.

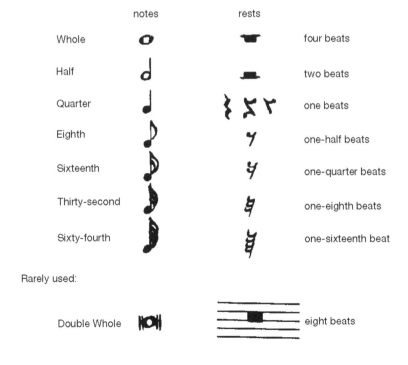

	notes	rests	
Whole	O	⬤	four beats
Half	♩	▬	two beats
Quarter	♩	❴	one beats
Eighth	♪	ǎ	one-half beats
Sixteenth	♬	ǎ	one-quarter beats
Thirty-second	♬	ǎ	one-eighth beats
Sixty-fourth	♬	ǎ	one-sixteenth beat

Rarely used:

Double Whole   IOI   ▬   eight beats

Relative duration of notes in terms of beats

Since only those tones whose relative duration can be expressed in multiples of two are possible with individual notes and rests, it is necessary to supplement these symbols with some device for extending their duration. One symbol used to extend the duration of a note is the *tie*. With the tie the total duration is extended to equal that of all notes connected by it:

Another device used to extend duration is the *dot*. A dot placed after a note increases its duration by one half.

Dotted notes

$$\text{♩.} = \text{♩} + \text{♪} \quad ; \quad \text{♪.} = \text{♪} + \text{♪}$$

Dots are also used to extend the duration of rests. There are times, however, when undotted rests are used to take the place of dotted ones when the meaning is clear. This is never done with notes.

The duration of a note or a rest may be further increased by one or more additional dots placed after the first. Each additional dot increases the duration by one-half of the previous dot.

Multiple-dotted notes and rests

Since the division of beats into small fractions is both difficult and impractical, it is useful to remember that dotted notes are most often written in conjunction with the short note or notes which make up the balance of the unit of duration:

Duration groups

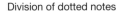

Dotted notes are divisible in the same manner as undotted ones, namely by two and multiples of two:

Division of dotted notes

Robert Schumann

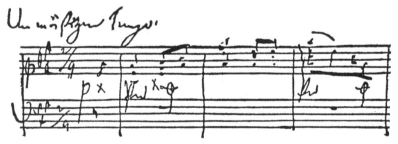

"Ländliches Lied" from No. 20, Album for the Young

Chapter 3

Meter

Sing the familiar tune "America," commonly known as "My Country, 'Tis of Thee," paying attention to the natural flow of the melody.

Examine the same melody now that the accented pulsations are indicated.

In any melody certain notes will be relatively more important than others. These more important notes seem to have more weight or accent than do the notes of lesser importance. This accent generally reoccurs with regularity. In notation we indicate the recurring accent by placing a *bar line* in front of the accented note.

That material which occurs between two bar lines is called a *measure.*

Accents occur not only with regularity, but also at greater or smaller intervals of time. This produces measures of various lengths. Contained in each measure will be the accented note followed by the notes of lesser importance. These patterns of strong and weak accents have a regular pulsation for a background. We call these pulsations *beats.* When we pat our feet or march to a piece of music we are expressing this background of beat.

This recurring pattern of accented and unaccented pulsations is known as *meter.* The same kind of meter is generally used throughout a piece or section of music, and in order to make this clear to the performer, we indicate the meter at the beginning of the composition by means of a *meter signature,* commonly referred to as a *time signature.* The meter signature consists of two figures placed one above the other and is written on the staff after the key signature, which will be discussed later.

Meter Signature

The meter signature, then, outlines the size of the measures in the piece. The lower figure indicates the kind of note and the upper figure the number in each measure. For example, in $\frac{2}{4}$ meter the measure contains two quarter notes or the equivalent. In $\frac{6}{8}$ meter the measure contains six eighth notes or the equivalent.

When each beat of a measure is normally divisible by two,

the meter is called *simple*. The following are examples of simple meter.

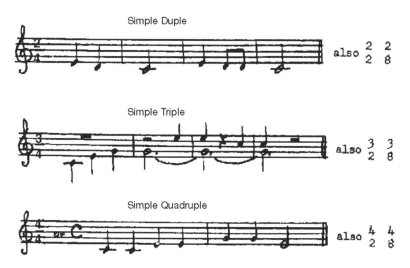

When each beat of a measure is normally divisible by three, the meter is called *compound*. The following are examples of compound meter.

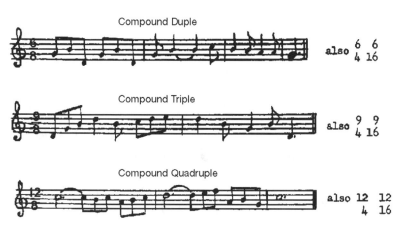

Rhythm

Rhythm is a term used broadly to mean the continuous flow of music. Normally we feel this as an organization of accents. If the accents appear more or less regularly, we say that the music is *metrical,* or that it can be written in measures. However, the rhythmic pattern does not necessarily coincide with the meter. The relation between the rhythmic pattern and the meter can be of three sorts:

a. Uniform, in which the note values coincide with the meter signature (or are in uniform divisions of the beat value);

b. Regular, in which the long notes coincide with the strong beats, and the shorter notes (when not uniform) occur on the weak beats;

c. Irregular, or syncopated, in which the long notes occur on weak beats or fractions of beats.

Occasionally in marches, fox trots, or other music in which there is a considerable feeling of motion, the composer will use the meter signature $\math{C}$, *Alla breve*, instead of the usual $\frac{4}{4}$ or C. In this meter the half note gets the beat rather than the quarter note, and it becomes $\frac{2}{2}$ instead of $\frac{4}{4}$.

Usually, when a piece begins with an incomplete measure the balance of the duration is found in the last bar of the piece. This fractional part of a beat or bar commonly referred to as a "pick-up" or "up-beat" is called the *anacrusis*. A phrase which begins on the first beat of a measure, on the "down-beat", is said to have a *thetic* beginning. These words are derived from the Greek terms, *arsis* and *thesis*, which, in poetry, refer to the weak and strong accents of a line.

Recently, however, some composers have adopted the practice of ending a piece with a complete bar regardless of the material contained in the first measure.

Subdivision

Quite often when performing music in which there are difficult rhythmic patterns it is helpful to further divide the beats into smaller units of duration. This is known as *subdivision*. Several examples of rhythms in which subdivision might be effective follow:

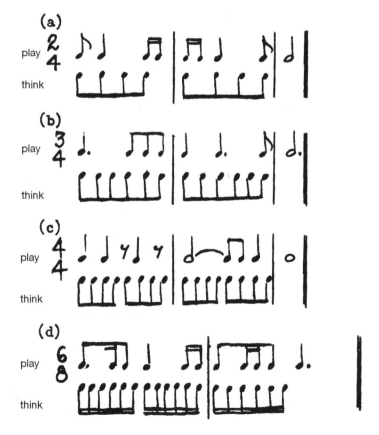

The student should remember that one meter can contain measures equal in duration to those of another meter. One performance would be correct; the other, incorrect. The meter signature will always make this distinction clear. It is necessary to "feel" the flow of the music when in doubt. Here is a familiar tune which, except for the meter signature would be equally playable two ways:

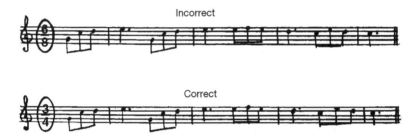

Frederic Chopin

From Prelude in E Minor, Op. 28, No. 4

Intervals

An interval is the relation of two tones with respect to their difference in pitch. When the two tones are sounded together the interval is said to be *harmonic*, and when sounded in succession the interval is said to be *melodic*.

In our system of music the smallest distance between two pitches is called a *half step* or *semi-tone*, two of which are equal to a *whole step* or *whole-tone*.

The distance from any pitch of a given letter-name to the next higher or lower pitch with the same letter-name is called an *octave*.

On the staff the interval of an octave includes eight lines and spaces or letter-names, hence the name, octave.

The number-name of intervals is always determined by the number of letter-names included in its formation, including the first and the last.

unison
or   2nd   3rd   4th   5th   6th   7th
prime

If we look back at the overtone series which we saw earlier we notice that the fundamental and the first overtone form the interval of an octave.

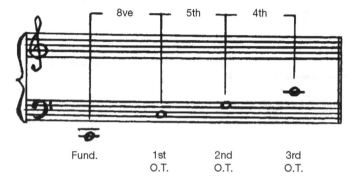

We also notice that the interval between the first and second overtones includes five lines and spaces. This interval is called a *fifth*. And in like manner, the next interval is called a *fourth*.

These three intervals are the most fundamental ones in nature and make up the foundation of our system of pitch relationships. The octave, fifth, and fourth as they occur in the overtone series as well as the *unison* or *prime*, are called *perfect*, and when speaking of them they are referred to as the *perfect octave, perfect fifth, perfect fourth*, and the *perfect prime*.

If one sings the opening few bars of the song, "Swanee River," paying particular attention to the word "Swanee," he will discover the interval of a perfect octave.

Likewise, on singing the familiar tune "Twinkle, Twinkle Little Star," one will discover that between the words "twinkle, twinkle," the interval is a perfect fifth.

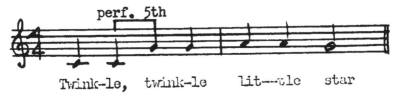

The perfect fourth may be found in the opening phrase of "Auld Lang Syne."

Using the idea of "discovery" one can sing through many familiar melodies and find not only the three perfect intervals, but many more. Of the remaining possibilities, several occur more frequently than the others and have been given names according to their size.

The major third (four half steps) as found in "Anchors Aweigh":

The major sixth (nine half steps) as found in "My Bonnie":

The major second (two half steps) as found in "Yankee Doodle":

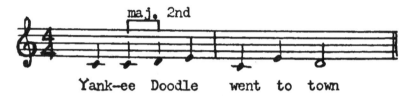

The major seventh (11 half steps) occurs infrequently by itself but quite often is found in combination with other intervals.

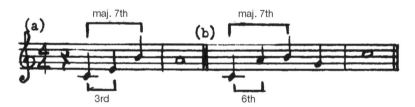

When all of these intervals are grouped together and arranged according to size from the smallest to the largest, the resulting pattern is known as the *major scale*. Scales will be discussed fully in the next chapter.

| perf. unison or prime | maj. 2nd | maj. 3rd | perf. 4th | perf. 5th | maj. 6th | maj. 7th | perf. 8th |

Any note may be used as a starting point, and by arranging the ascending line according to this pattern the student is provided with a convenient way to learn recognition of intervals.

These intervals are known as *diatonic intervals.* When any of the diatonic intervals are either compressed or enlarged, they become *chromatic intervals.* These changes in pitch are represented by the use of *accidentals* which are placed immediately in front of the note to be affected.

The Five Accidentals

Double-sharp	𝄪	Raises the pitch of the letter-name one whole step
Sharp	♯	Raises the pitch of the letter-name one half step
Natural	♮	Returns the tone to the pitch of the letter-name
Flat	♭	Lowers the pitch of the letter-name one half step
Double-flat	♭♭	Lowers the pitch of the letter-name one whole step

An *accidental* affects the note before which it stands and also the succeeding ones on the *same* line or space in the measure in which it occurs. The succeeding measures are not affected, but when the note of the same letter-name occurs in its natural form in a measure immediately following its altered form, it is best to *clarify* this return by the use of the natural sign.

If an accidental is to apply to a note of the same letter-name but on a different line or space, it should be indicated by the use of another accidental.

Table of Chromatic Intervals

PERFECT INTERVALS

Interval	Diatonic	Compressed 1/2 step		Enlarged 1/2 step	
	Perfect	Diminished		Augmented	
Prime					
Fourth					
Fifth					
Octave					

MAJOR INTERVALS

Interval	Diatonic	Compressed 1/2 step	Compressed whole step		Enlarged 1/2 step
	major	minor	diminished		augmented
Second					
Third					
Sixth					
Seventh					

When a diminished interval is compressed by ¹/₂ step it becomes doubly diminished. When an augmented interval is enlarged by ¹/₂ step it becomes doubly augmented.

Enharmonic Intervals

Some intervals may be notated two ways:

It would be impossible by sound alone to determine which was the correct notation. When the same pitches are representable on the staff by different letter names, the tones are said to be *enharmonic.* Enharmonic notation is usually the result of melodic or harmonic movement, which is dealt with more fully in the study of harmony.

Thus far we have mentioned only those intervals which are contained within the space of an octave; these are called *simple intervals. Compound intervals* are intervals larger than an octave. They become extremely important when studying part writing and voice leading.

Inversion of Intervals

Sometimes the range of a voice or instrument or other consideration makes it necessary to change the relative position of the tones in an interval. What usually happens is that the interval becomes inverted. An interval is said to be inverted either when the lower note becomes the upper or when the upper note becomes the lower. Given F to C (perfect fifth), in order for inversion to take place either F is placed above C or C is placed below F.

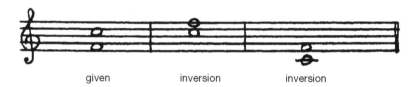

given   inversion   inversion

It will be noticed that perfect intervals remain perfect upon inversion; while majors become minor and minors become major; augmenteds become diminished, and diminisheds, augmented. The sum of the interval and its inversion is always nine: an octave becomes a unison; a third becomes a sixth; a fourth, a fifth; and so on.

Johann Sebastian Bach

Opening Measures of the First Prelude in Book 1,
Well-Tempered Clavichord

Morning Prayers in the Bach Family

Scales

A *scale* (Ital. *scala*-ladder) is a pattern of consecutive ascending or descending tones within the compass of an octave.

The Major Scale

In the opening measures of the familiar hymn tune, "Joy to the World," we find an arrangement of tones seen earlier in our study of intervals.

While singing the example pay particular attention to the distribution of whole and half steps in pattern (a), then in patterns (b) and (c). A group of four tones on successive degrees of the staff is called a *tetrachord.* (The student must not confuse the term tetrachord with chord.) On analysis of the tetrachord (d) we find that it consists of two whole steps and a half step, expressed as 1-1-$^1/_2$. Tetrachords are always figured from the bottom tone upward. A tetrachord built according to this pattern is called a *major tetrachord.* Then with the addition of the tetrachord (e), which we find also to be a major tetrachord, the scale is completed. Thus, a combination of two major tetrachords, separated by a whole step, produces a *major scale.* A major scale can be built on any pitch, for example:

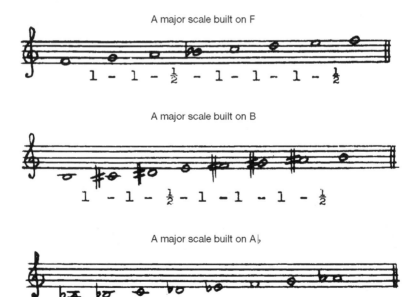

A major scale built on F

1 - 1 - $\frac{1}{2}$ - 1 - 1 - 1 - $\frac{1}{2}$

A major scale built on B

1 - 1 - $\frac{1}{2}$ - 1 - 1 - 1 - $\frac{1}{2}$

A major scale built on A♭

1 - 1 - $\frac{1}{2}$ - 1 - 1 - 1 - $\frac{1}{2}$

The Minor Scale

The minor scale has three separate forms, each designed for use in situations where the music requires special treatment either in the melody or harmony. Each of the minor scales is made up of a combination of two of these four tetrachords:

Each tetrachord should be sung and analyzed according to distribution of whole and half steps. We find the tetrachord at (a) to be a *major tetrachord* (1-1- $^1/_2$). The pattern at (b), (1-$^1/_2$-1) we call a *minor tetrachord*. A tetrachord built according to pattern (c), ($^1/_2$-1-1) is a *natural tetrachord*, and (d), ($^1/_2$-1$^1/_2$-$^1/_2$) is known as a *harmonic tetrachord*.

In the illustrations, half steps are indicated by a short curved line. The rest of the tones are understood to be a whole step apart. The step and a half is indicated with a bracket (—).

Natural minor scale

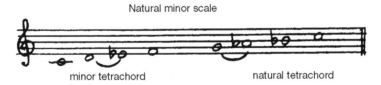

minor tetrachord   natural tetrachord

Sing a minor tetrachord. One whole step above the last note sing a *natural* tetrachord. The result is the "natural minor scale." This scale is also known as the "original minor," "pure minor," and "aeolian mode."

Melodic minor scale

ascending   descending

minor tetrachord   major tetrachord   natural tetrachord   minor tetrachord

Sing a minor tetrachord. One whole step above the last note sing a *major* tetrachord. The result is the ascending form of the "melodic minor scale." Beginning on the last note of the major tetrachord sing (descending) a *natural* tetrachord. One whole step lower complete with a *minor* tetrachord. The result is the descending form of the "melodic minor scale." It must be remembered that this scale has both an ascending and a descending form.

Harmonic minor scale

minor tetrachord   harmonic tetrachord

Sing a minor tetrachord. One whole step above the last note sing a *harmonic* tetrachord. The result is the "harmonic minor scale." The harmonic minor scale is the one usually intended when speaking of minor scales. The melodic and natural minor scales should be identified by name when referring to them.

Minor scales can also be built on any pitch provided that the appropriate tetrachords are used and that they are separated by a whole step. For example:

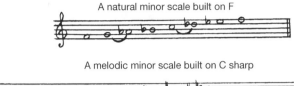

A natural minor scale built on F

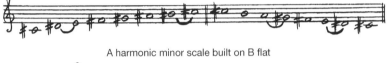

A melodic minor scale built on C sharp

A harmonic minor scale built on B flat

A summary of tetrachords as used in the major and minor scales:

Scale	Lower tetrachord		Upper tetrachord
Major	Major ——— Whole step ——→		Major
Minor			
Natural	Minor	"	Natural
Melodic ascending	Minor	"	Major
Melodic descending	Minor	"	Natural
Harmonic	Minor	"	Harmonic

Names of the Scale Degrees

The degrees of the scale have special names which are always used when referring to them. In a scale built on C they would be:

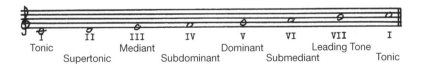

I	II	III	IV	V	VI	VII	I
Tonic		Mediant		Dominant		Leading Tone	Tonic
	Supertonic		Subdominant		Submediant		

Scale Degree Activity

Rest tones (i.e., the 1st, 3rd, and 5th scale degrees) have a tendency to remain stationary. *Active tones* (i.e., the 2nd, 4th, 6th, and 7th scale degrees) are very active and tend to move to the nearest rest tone.

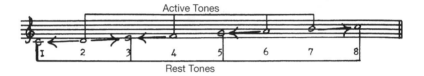

Key Signatures

To save unnecessary writing, the essential sharps or flats occurring in these scales are placed at the beginning of a piece of music immediately after the clef sign and on their proper lines or spaces. This arrangement of the accidentals at the beginning of a piece is called the *key signature.* An accidental in the key signature affects all notes of that letter-name, at all octaves, throughout the piece, unless changed by another accidental.

The order in which the sharps occur is F, C, G, D, A, E, and B. They are placed on the staff in that order according to the following pattern:

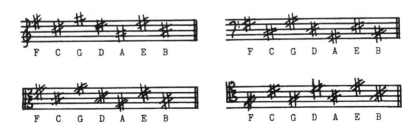

The flats occur in exactly the reverse order: B, E, A, D, G, C, and F and are placed on the staff as follows:

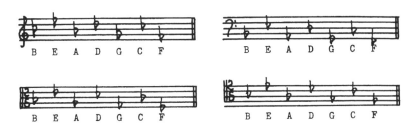

Key signatures are not only recognizable to the performer by the number of flats or sharps contained in them but also by the order and general shape of the group of flats or sharps. For these reasons it is necessary to use care in writing key signatures, keeping the group neatly spaced. The correct key signatures follow along with the keynote of each.

The key signatures

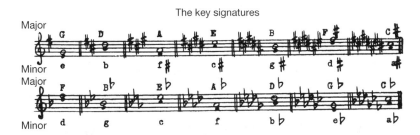

Individual accidentals which occur during the piece affect only the pitches of those lines or spaces on which they occur, and only within that measure. The key signature of the piece is always in effect after a bar line except in the case of a note tied to an altered note in the previous bar.

Relative and Parallel Scales

When two scales have the same tones and the same key signatures they are said to be *relative scales*.

C minor is said to be the relative minor of E♭ major. E♭ major is said to be the relative major of C minor.

When a major and a minor scale are written with the same key-note they are closely related because they have the same tonic and dominant. The minor scale is called the *tonic* or *parallel* minor. When using the melodic or harmonic minor scales it is necessary to write in the accidentals that affect the sixth and seventh degrees of the scale since the key signature is for the natural minor only. Pay particular attention to the key signatures of the following scales.

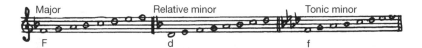

Chromatic Scales

As we said earlier, if we count all of the notes that can fit into the octave, the total is twelve. It is possible to construct any of the scales we have learned so far on any one of these pitches. If all twelve tones are played in an ascending or a descending order the result is a *chromatic scale*.

The traditional way of writing chromatic scales, up to the latter part of the nineteenth century, was to employ notes occurring in closely related scales. If this is done, in writing an ascending chromatic major scale the sixth degree would not be raised, and in the descending chromatic major scale the fifth degree would not be lowered.

The student will see that, in order to follow this method of notation consistently, the key that the music is written in must, at all times, be clearly defined. With the advent of chromatic harmonies and shifting tonalities, this method of notating the chromatic scale became obsolete. Today, the composer uses another method of writing chromatics. The diatonic scale steps are kept intact and the chromatic scale steps are obtained by raising all diatonic notes when ascending, and lowering all diatonic notes when descending.

In actual practice chromatic scales are often notated in the simplest or most convenient way. In the following example the two scales sound alike and both are notated correctly, but the performer is likely to find the second one easier to read than the first, because the second scale uses notes with which he or she is more familiar.

The constant use of a great many double-sharps or double-flats can very often be avoided by a change of key signature.

It should be remembered that what has been said regarding the building of chromatic scales applies not only to the full scale of an octave but also to any small portion of it such as from one scale degree to another.

Modes

The music that we are concerned with was written principally in the eighteenth and nineteenth centuries. The major and the minor scales were the predominant scales used in that period. However, before this period composers wrote in what are known as modes (different types of scales). Each mode had a traditional Greek name. Here are examples of some of the modes which were used during the fifteenth and sixteenth centuries.

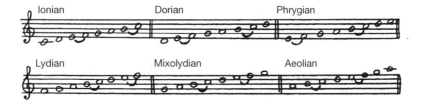

Other Scales .

There are actually several hundred types of scales and a study of these, or even a listing, would take an entire book. Also, many of them are not representable in our system of notation. However, a few scales the student may run across in his or her studies, are listed below.

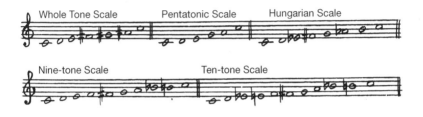

Circle of Keys

The following chart is called the *circle of keys* or the *circle of fifths.* In using this chart, which gives all of the signatures for the different major and minor keys, the student should note, in going around the circle clockwise, that the tonic of each sharp key is a fifth (five notes) higher that the tonic of the preceding key; in going around the circle counterclockwise, the tonic of each flat key is a fifth lower than the tonic of the proceeding one.

Capital letters indicate the names of the major keys; small letters indicate the minor keys.

The tonic of the major key is indicated by a whole note; the tonic of the minor key, by the head of a quarter note.

The enharmonic keys are connected by a line. Two keys, which are enharmonically related, will have the same sound for the corresponding scale degrees, but these corresponding scale degrees will be written differently.

Ludwig Van Beethoven

From Sonata. Op. 26

Beethoven's House in Vienna

CIRCLE OF KEYS

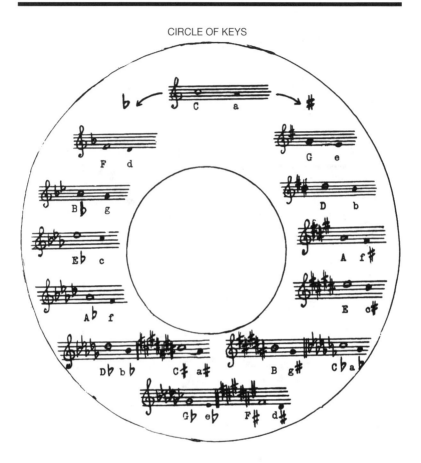

Refer to previous page for explanation of this chart

Transposition

It is sometimes necessary to write, read, or perform a piece of music in a key other than that in which it was originally written. This process of reproducing a piece of music at a different pitch is called *transposition*.

Clef

We explained earlier that a clef is a device for indicating some five-line portion of the great staff: that is, by means of clefs we can actually change the letter-names of the lines and spaces of the five-line staff. We will illustrate how this is done by an example:

The following piece of music is to be transposed a major third higher than written.

We arrive at the tonic of the new key and its proper signature, in this case, the key of D major with its signature of two sharps.

We find the clef which will give the proper letter-name to the notes originally written in the key of B♭.

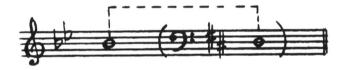

We make whatever changes are necessary in the accidentals used. In this case, the two accidentals used (naturals) *raised* the pitch of the notes following them, so in the new key we must use accidentals (sharps) which will also *raise* the degrees of the new key.

Here is another example. We will transpose this melody a perfect fourth lower. A perfect fourth lower than A major, is E major with its signature of four sharps. The tenor clef will be used because this gives us E on the fifth line. In transposing by clef we do not consider the correct *octave* for the new key, only the correct letter-names of the notes. The first accidental used (natural) *lowers* the tone following it; all of the other accidentals (sharps) *raise* the succeeding tones.

The system of transposing by clef is the most useful system of transposition, provided the student reads all of the clefs *fluently.* It is the *least* useful if he reads these clefs with difficulty.

Interval

When the difference between the old and the new key is small, i.e., a third or less, it is sometimes easier to transpose by thinking of the interval relationship of the two keys. The following melody is to be read one whole tone higher than written.

The student, then, thinks something like this:

One whole tone higher than A♭ is B♭

"	"	"	"	"	G	"	A
"	"	"	"	"	F	"	G
"	"	"	"	"	E	"	F#
"	"	"	"	"	F	"	G
"	"	"	"	"	D♭	"	E♭
"	"	"	"	"	C	"	D
"	"	"	"	"	A	"	B
"	"	"	"	"	B♭	"	C

In transposing by this method it is necessary to be extremely careful as far as accidentals are concerned, since the exact interval difference must be maintained at all times. The student may find it more practical to use this system in combination with the following one.

Scale Degree

In using this method of transposition the student relates the different degrees of the scale to a tonic by means of numbers. Here is an example:

The following melody, written in the key of C major, is to be transposed to the key of A♭ major. We first get the signature of the new key clearly in mind, in this case the signature of A♭ major, (4 flats).

The melody begins on the fifth degree of the scale (dominant) and goes to the first (tonic). In the key of C major this is G up to C; in the key of A♭ major this is E♭ up to A♭. Here are all of the scale degrees in the original key.

Then we substitute notes in the key of A♭ major for these scale degrees.

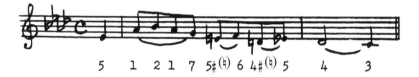

For the inexperienced student it is easier to transpose by a combination of interval and scale degree methods. He or she will read a piece of music at the required interval but will keep in mind the new signature and relate each tone to the tonic of the new key.

Change of Signature

When the transposition is one half step higher or lower this can sometimes be accomplished by mentally changing the key signature. For example, this melody has to be played one half step lower than written.

This is easily done by imagining the signature of G♭ major and playing the same written notes.

To transpose one half step higher the following melody in that key of B♭ major, we would use the signature of B major.

One half step higher

In transposing by any of the above methods the student may at first have difficulty whenever encountering accidentals. The student must first analyze *what* the original accidental did in the old key (whether it *raised* or *lowered* a note), and then duplicate this in the new key. The *same kind* of accidental may not always be used in both keys, but the *operation* of the accidental must always be the same.

Chapter 7
Musical Instruments

Names and Pitches of Musical Instruments

The purpose of this chapter is not to outline a study of instrumentation, but rather to provide the student with such basic knowledge as is thought to be of practical everyday importance.

Musical instruments are divided into four principal classifications: strings, winds, percussion, and keyboard instruments. Wind instruments are further divided into woodwinds and brass.

(a) String instruments in common use are

Violin	treble clef; sounds as written.
Viola	alto and treble clefs; sounds as written.
Cello	bass, tenor, and occasionally the treble clef; sounds as written.
Bass (string bass, contra bass, double bass)	bass and tenor clefs; sounds an octave lower than written.

(b) Woodwinds in common use are

C Flute	treble clef; sounds as written.
C Piccolo	treble clef; sounds an octave higher than written.
D♭ Piccolo	treble clef; sounds one octave plus $1/2$ step higher than written.
Oboe	treble clef; concert instrument, sounds as written.
English Horn in F	treble clef; sounds a perfect fifth lower than written.
Bassoon	bass and tenor clefs; concert instrument, sounds as written.
E♭ Clarinet	treble clef; sounds minor third higher than written.
B♭ Clarinet	treble clef; sounds whole step lower than written.
E♭ Alto Clarinet	treble clef; sounds major sixth lower than written.
B♭ Bass Clarinet	treble clef; sounds an octave plus whole step lower than written. (One octave lower than B♭ Clarinet)
E♭ Alto Saxophone	treble clef; sounds a major sixth lower than written.
B♭ Tenor Saxophone	treble clef; sounds an octave plus a whole step lower than written.
E♭ Baritone Saxophone	treble clef; sounds an octave and a major sixth lower than written. (One octave lower than Alto Saxophone)

(c) Brass instruments in common use are

B♭ Cornet,	treble clef; sounds a whole step lower
B♭ Trumpet	than written.
F Horn	treble clef; sounds a perfect fifth lower than written.
E♭ Alto Horn	treble clef; sounds a major sixth lower than written.
B♭ Tenor Trombone	bass and tenor clefs; concert instrument, sounds as written.
B♭ Bass Trombone	bass clef; concert instrument, sounds as written.
Baritone Horn	bass and tenor clefs; concert instrument, sounds as written.
E♭ Tuba/ Sousaphone	bass clef; concert instruments, sound as written.
BB♭ Tuba/ Sousaphone	bass clef; concert instruments, sound as written.

(d) Percussion instruments in common use are

Snare Drum	third space bass clef; indefinite pitch.
Bass Drum	first space bass clef; indefinite pitch.
Cymbals	written with drum parts; indefinite pitch.
Triangle	written with drum parts; indefinite pitch.
Timpani	bass clef; sounds as written.
Glockenspiel and Bell Lyre	treble clef; sound as written.
Xylophone	treble clef; sounds as written.

(e) Keyboard instruments in common use are

Piano	treble and bass clefs; sounds as written.
Organ	treble and bass clefs plus additional staff for pedals; sounds as written.
Celeste	treble and bass clefs; sounds an octave higher than written.

(f) Miscellaneous instruments in common use are

Harp	treble and bass clefs; sounds as written.
Guitar	treble clef plus chord symbols; sounds one octave lower than written.

Ranges of Band Instruments

A list of common band instruments, together with the practical range of each, follows. It must be remembered that reed and brass instrumental ranges are limited, to a large extent, by the performer as well as by the instrument, and that the ranges given here are representative of the average-to-good Armed Service instrumentalists and not the extreme ranges of some soloists.

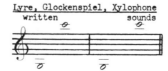

George Friedrich Handel

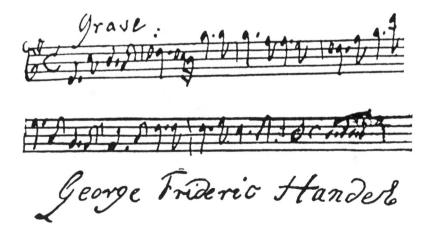

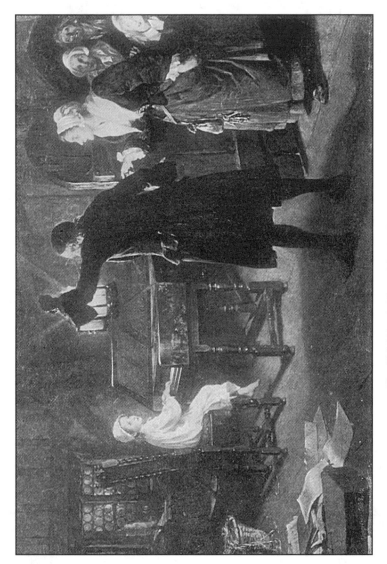

The Child Handel Practicing in the Attic

Chapter 8

Directions for Performance (part I)

A large portion of the music for band is inherited from the orchestral literature of the 18th and 19th centuries. Most of this music is of European origin and reflects the traditional practice of expressing directions for performance in Italian. In order to understand these words or phrases, the performer must be able to translate them into English. In the sections that follow, the words found most often in the band repertoire have been selected and their translation given.

There is a certain group of small words which occur frequently and are used to connect and modify the principal words. The most common of these follow, along with their translations. Additional words may be found in the glossary in the back of the book.

Word	*Translation*
a	in, by, at
assai	very
bis	again
con	with
doppio	double
e	and
il	the

Word	Translation
ma	but
meno	less
mezzo	half
molto	much, very
mosso	moving
moto	motion
non	not
Piu	more
poco	little
primo	first
quasi	like, as, in the manner or style of
sempre	always, continually
sotto	under, below
stesso	same
stretto	drawn together, in faster tempo
sul	on
tanto	as much, so much
tenuto	held full value
troppo	too much
un, uno, una	a, an, one
voce	voice

These words are sometimes found together in phrases. Several typical examples follow:

ma non troppo	but not too much
poco a poco	little by little
un poco meno (forte)	a little less (loud)
molto piu	much more
non tanto	not as much, not so much
con moto	with motion

Dynamic Indications

Those terms and signs which deal with intensity are called *dynamic indications.* The most common of these follow, along with their translations.

Words Indicating Level of Intensity:

Word	Abbreviation or Symbol	Translation
Pianissimo	pp	very soft
Piano	p	soft
Mezzo piano	mp	half or medium soft
Mezzo forte	mf	half or medium strong or loud
Forte	f	strong or loud
Fortissimo	ff	very strong or loud

The above list of words contains two words which end in -issimo. This suffix is a superlative which intensifies the meaning. Its literal translation is "most," however it is not uncommon to substitute the term "very" as in pianissimo: Piano, meaning soft; Pianissimo, meaning most softly or very soft. The same holds true with the word fortissimo: Forte, meaning strong; Fortissimo, meaning very strong, and so on. Another example of a suffix which is often seen in music is –etto. This suffix tends to lessen the intensity of the word and is therefore called a diminutive. The term Largo, meaning large, broad, wide, and so on, would be lessened somewhat as Larghetto and would become less large, less broad, less wide, and so on.

The student must be careful to understand the correct meaning of the stem or principal part of the word in order to give the proper interpretation to the combination. For example: if the principal part of the word means "slow," then the addition of -issimo would mean "very slow." Likewise, the addition of -etto would mean "less slow." On the other hand, if the principal part of the word means "fast," then the addition of -issimo would mean "very fast" and -etto, "less fast."

Words Indicating Change in the Level of Intensity

Word	*Abbreviation*	*Translation*
Calando	cal.	decreasing in loudness, slowing
Crescendo	cresc.	increasing in loudness (gradually)
Decrescendo	decresc., dec.	decreasing in loudness (gradually)
Diminuendo	dim.	decreasing in loudness (gradually)
Forzando, forzato	fz	accenting strongly
Sforzando, sforzato	sfz	forced, reinforced, strongly accented
Morendo	mor.	decreasing in loudness, slowing
Rinforzando	rfz, rinf.	sudden stress or emphasis
Smorzando	smorz.	decreasing in loudness, slowing

Tempo

61

Tempo

In the chapter on meter we said that tempo is the rate of speed at which music is played. Tempo may be indicated in terms of beat units per minute:

♩ = 120 indicates 120 half notes per minute

♩ = 90 indicates 90 quarter notes per minute

♩. = 60 indicates 60 dotted quarters per minute,

and so on. The settings on the metronome are in beats per minute.

Frequently there is some word or phrase at the beginning of a piece which gives a general indication of the tempo. The most common of these follow along with their translations.

Slow Tempos

Word	*Translation*	*Meaning in Music*
Largo	large, broad, wide, spacious	a very slow movement
Lento	slow	faster than largo
Adagio	slow, at ease, comfortably	faster than lento

Medium Tempos

Word	*Translation*	*Meaning in Music*
Andante	walking, going along	a moderate tempo
Moderato	in moderate time	a moderate tempo

Fast Tempos

Word	Translation	Meaning in Music
Allegretto	cheerful	faster than moderato
Allegro	quick, cheerful	faster than allegretto
Presto	very quick, fast	faster than allegro
Prestissimo	as fast as possible	extremely fast

Sometimes it is necessary to indicate changes of tempo during a piece. The most common words indicating changes of tempo follow, along with their translations.

For increasing the tempo:

Accelerando	accelerating
Incalzando	hastening, pressing forward
Stringendo	quickening, accelerating
Piu mosso	more moving, more motion

For decreasing the tempo:

Allargando	becoming broader, slower
Calando	slowing and decreasing in loudness
Rallentando (rall.)	gradually slower
Ritardando (rit.)	same as *rallentando*
Ritenuto	suddenly slower
Meno mosso	less moving, less motion
Morendo	slowing and decreasing in loudness
Smorzando	slowing and decreasing in loudness

For returning to previous tempos:

A tempo	in tempo, in original tempo
Primo tempo, tempo I	first tempo
Stesso tempo, l'istesso tempo	same tempo (as before)

Momentary Changes in Tempo:

Rubato	stolen, robbed, deliberate unsteadiness of tempo, a slackening and quickening of the tempo for sake of expression
Fermata	a pause, indicated by the sign ⌢ or hold
General Pause (G. P.)	a rest for the entire band, sometimes called Grand Pause
Lunga pausa	a long pause
Cut-off (//)	an immediate stop
Tenuto (ten.)	held full value

Special Tempo Markings:

𝅗𝅥 = 𝅘𝅥 ,   𝅘𝅥. = 𝅘𝅥 ,   𝅘𝅥 = 𝅘𝅥𝅮 , etc.

These signs are found at points in the music where the meter changes but the tempo remains constant. The first note in each case represents the beat unit in the first meter and the second note represents the new beat unit in the second meter. For example:

if 𝅗𝅥 = 120   and 𝅗𝅥 = 𝅘𝅥   then 𝅘𝅥 = 120.

The speed of half notes in the first tempo would be equal to the speed of quarter notes in the second tempo. Likewise, when 𝅘𝅥.‗𝅘𝅥 the speed of dotted half notes in the first tempo would equal the speed of undotted half notes in the second tempo.

𝅗𝅥 ‗ 𝅗𝅥 ,   𝅘𝅥 ‗ 𝅘𝅥 ,   𝅘𝅥. ‗ 𝅘𝅥. , etc.

In this case a specific note value in the first meter would be equal to the same note value in the second meter, regardless of the meter in either case. For example:

if $\half = 120$ and $\eighth = \eighth$ then $\half = 120$

The following example is notated two ways and the manner of performance indicated:

Performed {

Steady $\frac{2}{4}$ with triplet   Even quarters throughout

Character Markings

The particular character or mood of a piece is often expressed in some word or phrase either in conjunction with the tempo indication or independently at the beginning of the piece. A list of the most common character markings follows. Further words and phrases indicating character may be found in the glossary of terms in the back of the book.

Word	Translation
agitato	agitated, hurriedly
animato	animatedly, with spirit
bravura	courage, bravery, brilliance, virtuosity
brillante	brilliantly
brio	spirit, fire, brilliance
cantabile	singable, singing, lyrical
cantando	singing, as if sung
deciso	in a bold manner, decisively

dolce	sweetly and softly
dolore	grief, sorrowfully
energico	energetically
espressivo	with expression
forza	force; con forza-forcefully
fuoco	fire
giusto	just, strict, suitable (tempo giusto; strict time)
lacrimoso	tearfully, mournfully
legato	smoothly, in a flowing manner
leggiero	lightly
marcato	markedly, emphatically
marziale	martially, in a military manner
misterioso	in a mysterious manner
passionato, appassionato	impassioned
pesante	heavily, with marked emphasis
piacere, a piacere	agreeably, with pleasure
pomposo	with pomp, majestically
religioso	solemnly, religiously
scherzando	in a light, playful manner
sostenuto	sustained, drawn out
spiccato	distinctly, detached
strepitoso	very loudly, noisily
vigoroso	vigorously

Music in a Given Tradition

It should be remembered that along with the directions for performance of music there are certain traditional practices which tend to govern its interpretation. For example, music of Haydn would receive a performance quite unlike that of Verdi, even though on the printed page certain similarities might appear. The attitudes of the times in which these two men lived were quite different, and the music of the two periods reflects this difference. Not only were their performing groups of different size and instrumental make-up, but their entire concept of music (harmony, rhythm, and melody) differed in many ways.

Notation itself frequently gives some evidence of the customs and beliefs of the period. In some cases similar notation would receive different performances; likewise, similar performances could result from unlike notation. It is necessary to be familiar with such peculiarities if a performance of music of a given period or composer is to be in good taste.

Miscellaneous Terms and Signs

In instrumental music, words and signs are frequently found which are intended by the composer or arranger to further clarify the notation or give additional directions for performance. The most common of these follow, along with their translations and explanations:

attacca subito	to attack or begin what follows immediately
divisi (div.), a2	divided, to be played by two performers or groups of performers, in two parts, frequently follows section in which part is marked solo
col. part., colla parte	with the part, indicates that instrument is to perform with the part identified
segue	now follows, go on, continue
solo	alone, performed by single performer
soli	plural of solo, as when a group of performers plays solo parts
sordino, sordini (sord.)	mute, mutes
con sordino	with mute, muted
senze sordina	without mute
vibrato (vib.)	vibrating, a slight fluctuation of pitch
volta subito (v.s.)	turn immediately
tremolo (trem.)	trembling, reiteration with great rapidity
tutti	all, together, full band or section

Felix Mendelssohn Bartholdy

Chapter 9

Directions for Performance (part II)

Musical Abbreviations

In order to facilitate the reading of music and to save unnecessary duplication and inconvenience in copying and publishing, a system of abbreviations has been developed. Those abbreviations which are considered to be widely used and understood follow.

*The *tremolo* is played as fast as possible when the tempo is too rapid to play as written. In writing for percussion instruments, this is sometimes called a roll or trill.

The Cross-strokes and Oblique line with two dots

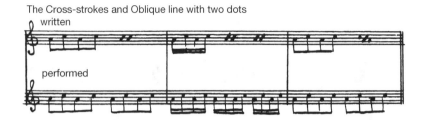

Repeated Measures and Double-Measures

Repeated Strains and Short Sections

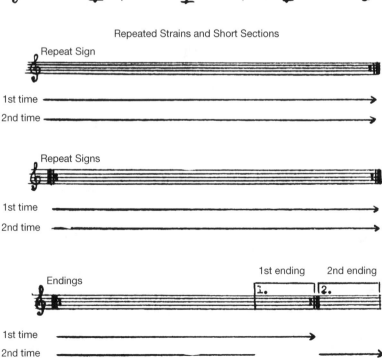

Repeated Sections

D.C. or *da capo* - from the head. Means to repeat from the beginning.

Fine - the end. Means the end of the piece or large section. Indicated by a double bar with a heavy line.

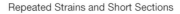

Repeated Strains and Short Sections

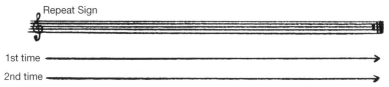

D.S. or *dal segno*-from the sign. Means to repeat from the sign (𝄋)

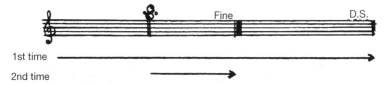

Coda sign (⊕). Used at point where skip is made to Coda and at Coda.

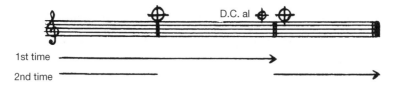

Octave Signs

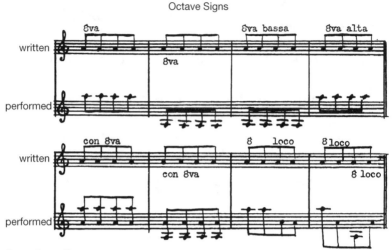

8va, 8ve, 8, ottava	= octave
8va bassa	= octave lower
8va alta	= octave higher
loco	= where written
con 8va	= with octave

Melodic Ornaments

In the 16th and 17th centuries, when the principal keyboard instruments were the harpsichord, clavichord, and spinet, composers decorated the melodies for these instruments with various ornaments and embellishments. This was done because these instruments had very little sustaining power. These elaborations made it possible to reiterate certain notes, thereby giving an illusion of sustained tone. Today, authorities differ as to the interpretation of the principal embellishments which are still used. There are, however, a few frequently used devices which receive a rather universal interpretation. The most common of these follow.

The Grace Note or Acciaccatura

A note in small type indicating that its time value is not counted in the rhythm of the measure and must be subtracted from one of the adjacent notes. It is usually performed *before* the beat, taking its time value from the *preceding* note and is very short.

As used in music of the Classic period, Haydn and Mozart for example, this grace note usually occurs *on* the beat, taking its time value from the *succeeding* note and is very short.

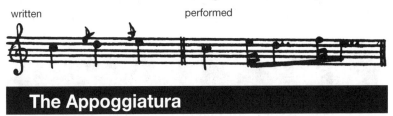

The Appoggiatura

A note also in small type whose time value is unaccounted for in the rhythm of the measure but which *always* occurs *on* the beat and takes its time value from the succeeding note as follows:

(a) If the appoggiatura precedes a note whose time value is divisible by *two* it receives *one-half* of the time value.

(b) If the appoggiatura precedes a note whose time value is divisible by *three*, it receives *two-thirds* of the time value.

The Double Grace Note

Two notes (usually one above and one below the principal note) which may be performed either *on* the beat or *before*, depending on the character of the music. The usual practice is to perform them *before* the beat.

The Slide

A scalewise series of two or more small notes usually performed *before* the beat although they are sometimes performed *on* the beat, depending on the character of the music.

The Mordent

A single, double, or triple alternation of the principal note with its upper or lower neighbor (note in scale one step above or below).

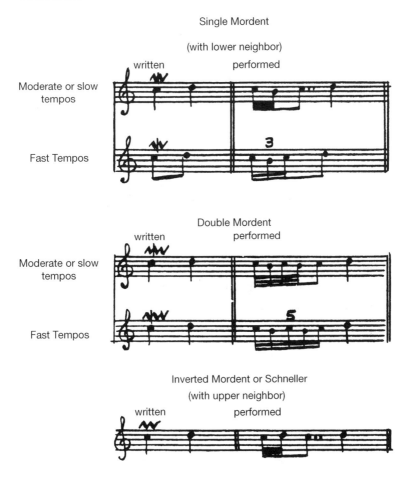

Single Mordent

(with lower neighbor)

Double Mordent

Inverted Mordent or Schneller

(with upper neighbor)

When an accidental applies, it is written above or below the sign.

written   performed

The Turn or Gruppetto

Directly over a note

written   performed

Occasionaly the turn is inverted

written   performed

Between two notes, a pause is made on the first principal note with the remaining tones being played rapidly without a break into the next principal note.

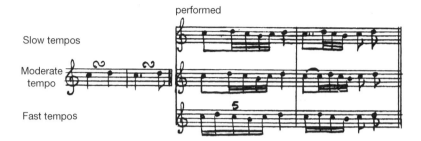

Between two notes of the same pitch

Accidentals which affect the neighboring tones are placed above or below the sign as appropriate.

The Trill

A rapid, even alternation of the principal note with its upper neighbor which lasts for the entire duration of the principal note, continuing to the end of the waved line.

Often a trill is followed by one or more short notes leading to the next long note.

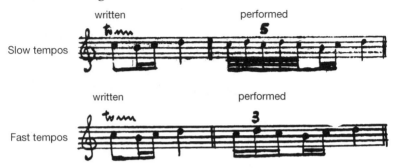

A trill may be followed by another note of the same pitch.

The trill note may be tied to a second note.

The number of notes in a trill varies with the tempo of the music.

Sometimes in solos a trill begins slowly and increases in tempo. This is called a progressive trill. There is no special notation for such a trill.

Accidentals which affect the neighboring tone being trilled are placed above the trill sign.

Trill with Upper Neighbor

The trill begins with the *upper neighbor* instead of the principal note under the following circumstances:

(a) In music of Bach's period.

(b) In Haydn, Mozart, and their contemporaries if the note preceding the principal note is the *same* note or a *lower* one.

(c) In more recent music when the upper neighbor is written as a grace note.

Special Articulations and Accents

When the composer or arranger intends that specific emphasis be applied to the performance of his music he or she uses a group of special signs. There is much controversy over the particular interpretation of many of these signs, due in large part to the indiscriminate use of them by some composers and to contrasting views among performers.

In any case the *style* and *character* of the music must be regarded as the essential determinants of performance, and any signs or other interpretation markings simply as safeguards or reminders.

In music for wind instruments in general and for the military band in particular, certain standards and practices have been adopted and show a rather universal acceptance.

Several common articulation markings and accents follow along with suggestions as to their probable performances.

Articulations

Legato - Slurred

Maximum duration. To be performed *without interruption* between notes. Only the first note is attacked.

Non legato - Leggiero

Slightly less than maximum duration. To be performed with a *slight break* between notes.

Mezzo-Staccato

Approximately half or slightly more than half of duration. To be performed with a break between notes.

Staccato

A lessening of duration usually about one-half. Performance varies from *short* to *very short* with the character and tempo of the music.

Staccatissimo

An extreme shortening of duration. Usually performed as short as possible with a slight emphasis in intensity.

Accents

Horizontal Accent

Attacked with force, usually followed by slight decrescendo. Performed louder than surrounding dynamic level. It has no effect on duration.

Vertical Accent

Attacked with force, usually followed by retention of dynamic level. Performed louder than surrounding dynamic level. Occasionally performed with slight lessening of duration.

Combinations

Frequently these signs are used in combinations, two common examples of which follow.

Example (a) is performed as a combination of staccato and vertical accent, while example (b) is performed as legato with individual attacks on each note.

Wolfgang Amadeus Mozart

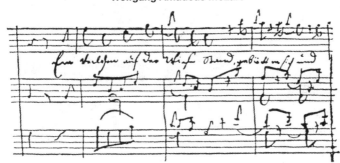

Mozart in Vienna

Chapter 10

Devices Peculiar to Dance Music

Rip or Flare

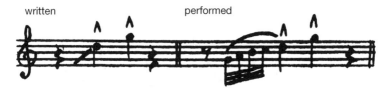

written   performed

A *rip* (called a *flare* in old stocks) is a fast glissando or slide preceding the principal note. A rip usually starts at least a fourth lower than the principal note and goes up diatonically. The interval started beneath the principal note and the time consumed by the rip is relative to the tempo, instrument, and register.

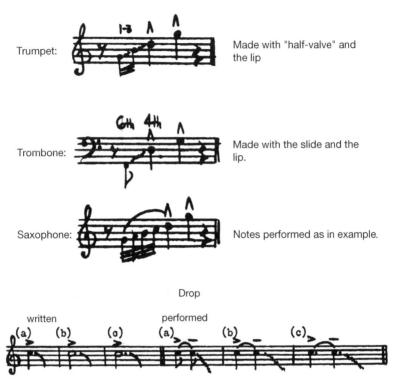

Trumpet:

Made with "half-valve" and the lip

Trombone:

Made with the slide and the lip.

Saxophone:

Notes performed as in example.

Drop

A drop is produced by making a fast glissando or slide down from the principal note. It may be diatonic, chromatic, or, in the brass, down through the harmonics. The drop is usually accompanied by a gradual relaxing of the embouchure, producing a "tailing off" and a vagueness of pitch on the end of the drop. The drop usually starts on the second half of the note and continues until the end of the note value.

The length and type of drop is relative to the tempo, note value, instrument, and register. Parts are usually marked if anything other than a regular fast diatonic drop is desired. The harmonic drop will cover the greatest interval.

Trumpet: The normal drop is made with half valves and the harmonic drop is made with just the lip.

Trombone: The normal drop is made with the slide, and the harmonic drop is made with just the lip.

Saxophone: The lip slide is impracticable on the saxophone (in comparison to valve or slide instruments). Saxophones use a combination of relaxing the embouchure and "coasting" their fingers down the keys. Saxophones are not as effective as brass on the long drops.

Bend

A *bend* (called a *smear* in old stocks) is produced by hitting under the pitch of the principal note and gradually bringing the tone up to the true pitch. The amount of bend and the time consumed in reaching the true pitch are relative to the tempo, the value of the note, and the register. The correct fingering or slide position for the principal note is used throughout the bend.

Trumpet, Trombone, and Saxophone as explained.

A *doink* is produced by tightening the embouchure after the attack and lip slurring up to the next octave, depending on the register. The total time consumed by the doink is usually that of the principal note.

Trumpet: Lip slur sometimes combined with half valve.
Trombone: Lip slur
Saxophone: Not too effective on saxophone because of the
             inability to raise the pitch to any appreciable
             degree. A substitute for a doink on a saxophone
             is a smooth upward "glissando slide."

A *scoop* is produced by slightly anticipating the principal
note with a slight bend. Somewhat like a bend on the lower
grace note.

Trumpet: Lip or "half-valve" grace note.
Trombone: Lip or slight slide movement.
Saxophone: Lip or a bend on the lower grace note.

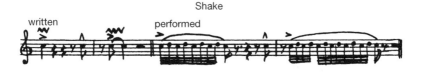

A shake is primarily a brass effect and is an unmeasured
lip trill from the principal note up to the next convenient harmonic. The shake is produced by an exaggerated hand vibrato
in conjunction with a lip trill. All shakes are fast unless otherwise marked.

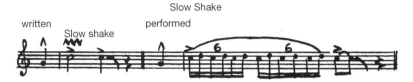

Slow Shake

written   performed

Slow shake

A *slow shake* is a more measured effect than the regular shake, and is produced solely by lip trilling.

The harmonic involved in the shake is relative to the register, valve combination (Trpt.), slide position (Trb.), etc. The speed of the shake is relative to the tempo, register, and markings.

Saxophone: The shake or lip trill can be made on only a very few notes on saxophone. These are made by a system of false fingerings, and are primarily used for solo work. A simulated shake can be produced on the saxophone by using a wide and exaggerated vibrato.

Muting

Open and Closed Brass Effects

+ – – – – – Bell closed with a plunger, hat, or hand.
0 – – – – – Bell opened.

One open and closed effect is attained by attacking each note and having the open and closed markings coincide with the attacks.

Another open and closed effect is attained by attacking just the first note of each group of notes and establishing the rhythm pattern by conforming to the open and closed markings.

Plunger: Technique easily acquired and very effective.

Hat: Different and interesting effect, but very awkward to use.

Hand: Very convenient, but not effective.

Rhythm

Eighth Notes

The usual dance interpretation of eighth notes.

Eighth notes which are to be played straight or even are marked as follows:

Each note is touched with a legato tongue without stopping the air stream.

The foregoing suggestions are recommended in the performance of stocks and "special arrangements" distributed by the U. S. Naval School of Music for use in authorized Navy Bands. The final interpretation of all markings is, however, up to the leader of the band or section.

False Notes

Playing *false* notes is more or less a playing of the rests. The false notes are usually very subdued, unaccented, and of a different timbre. They are produced by false fingerings on the saxophone; half-valve or false fingering on the trumpet; false slide positions on the trombone; or by a rolling of the tongue in the roof of the mouth on all instruments.

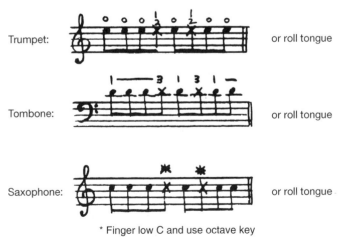

* Finger low C and use octave key

Abbreviations Used in Dance Music

Soli   The *lead* is in that section. The normal lead parts are lst alto, lst trumpet, and lst trombone. If the lead is in any other part it must be marked as being "lead."

For example: If all of the saxophone parts are marked "soli," then the lead is in the lst alto and the other saxophones are supporting the lst alto. If the lead for the soli is in the lst tenor part, this part is marked "lead," the lst alto, which normally has the lead, is marked "tenor lead" and the other saxophone parts are marked "soli."

N. V.   No Vibrato. This marking is necessary when the no vibrato sound is desired, because all parts, except unisons, are played with vibrato, under normal playing conditions.

W. V.   With Vibrato. Used to signify a return to the use of vibrato following a section marked N. V.

H. 0. B.   Hand Over Bell. A marking used in brass parts to minimize the "brassy" timbre of the instrument.

Sub Tone A saxophone and clarinet marking. The instrument is only partly filled with air, which tends to minimize the reediness of the tone.

X. 0.   Time (or Times) only. For example:

           IXO - - - - - -   lst time only.

           Play 3X - - - - Play three times.

           Solo 2XO - - - Solo second time only.

Ens.   Ensemble. The entire band (except rhythm) is playing the same line, in harmony, unless marked "Unison." The lead part in "ensembles" is always in the trumpet section.

Appendices

(A) Glossary of Terms

(B) Names of Musical Instruments in English, Italian, French, and German

(C) Form in Music with List of Terms

(D) Media

(E) Music Copying

(F) Conducting for Instrumentalists

(G) The 26 Essential Drum Rudiments

(H) Drum Majoring

(I) Dictionary of Musical Instruments

Franz Peter Schubert

Das Wandern.

(A) A Glossary of Additional Terms Found in Music for Band

accarezzevole – caressingly

accentuare – to accent

acciaccato – violently

addolorato – melancholy

adirato – angrily

affannato – tormented, distressed

affanoso – tormented, distressed

affetto – affection

affettuosamente – affecionately

afflizione – sorrow

aflitto – sorrowfully

affrettando – hurrying

affrettate– hurrying

affrettoso – hurried

agevole – agile

agevolmente – nimbly

aggiustatamente – in strict time

agiatamente – easily

agilita – agility

agitamento – agitation

agitazione – agitation

allegrezza – joy, cheer

allegria – joy, cheer

allentato – retarding

allentamento – retarding

allentando – retarding

allegrissimammente – extremely fast

allegrissimo– extremely fast

altra – another

altro – another

altra volta – encore

altro modo – alternate manner

amabilmente – amiably

amabilita – tenderness

amarezza – bitterness

amaro – bitterly

amorevole – lovingly

amoroso – lovingly

ancora – once more, yet, still

andantino – similar to andante (See p. 61)

andare diritto – go straight on

angoscia – anguish

appenato – distressed

ardente – ardently

ardentemente – ardently

articolazione – exact articulation

asprezza – harshness
assoluto – absolute
audace – audaciously
ballabile – in a dance manner
battuta – a beat
a battatura – with the beat, strictly in time
bellezza – beauty
bimmolle – the flat mark
biquadro – the natural sign
biscanto – a duet
bissare – encore
con bravura – with brilliancy
brilliante – brilliantly
brioso – with spirit; vivacity
con brio – with spirit; vivacity
calcando – animated
campanella – a little bell
capriccioso – capriciously
compiacevole – pleasantly
consolatamente – cheeringly
corrente – running
cupo – dark, reserved
delicatezza – delicacy
delicato – delicately
delirio – frenzy, excitement
deliberatamente – deliberately
desto – brisk, sprightly
devozione – devotion

di – of, with, for, from, by, etc.
da molto – extremely
diluendo – fading away
disaccentato – unaccented
disinvolto – easily
distinto – distinctly
divozione – devotion
deglia – grief
dolcemente –softly
doloroso – sorrowfully
dopo – after
due – two
enfasi – emphasis
entrata – an introduction
entusiasmo – enthusiasm
esecuzione – execution
espirando – dying away
estinto – hushed, all but silent
facilmente – with facility, in an easy manner
fantastico – fantastic, whimsical
fastoso – proudly, with a lofty style
feroce – fiercely, with ferocity
finito – concluded
fuocoso – with fire
franchezza – with freedom, boldly

gaio – gayly, cheerfully

gioioso –joyously

giustamente – with precision

indeciso – undecided

in fretta – in haste

inquieto – restless, uneasily

intrepidezza–with intrepidity

jubiloso – jubilantly

justo – just, precise

largamente – in a broad style

larghezza – in a broad style

larghissimo – extremely slow

lentando – with increased slowness

mancando – dying away

marcatissimo – very strongly marked

marcia funebre – a funeral march

martellando – strongly marking the notes

martellato – hammered

medessimo – the same

melodioso – melodiously

militarmente – in a military style

misurato – in a strict time

mobile – movable

mollemente – softly, gently

morendo – gradually slower

mormorando – murmuring

muta – change

nobile – with nobleness

nobilmente – with nobleness

ordinario – usual, common

partitura – the full score

pastorale – pastoral, rural

paventato – with an expression of anxiety

paventoso – with an expression of anxiety

per – for, by, through, in

perpetuo, – perpetual

piena – full

placido – placidly

pochettino – a very little

pochetto – a very little

ponderoso – ponderously

precisione – with precision

preciso – precise, exact

prestamente – rapidly

prestissimo – as fast as possible

prima volta – the first time

puntato – pointed, detached

rabbia – with rage, furiously

rapidamente – rapidly

rapido – rapidly

religiosamente – religiously

replicato – repeated

rigoroso – rigorous, exact time

rilasciando – relaxing the
time, giving way a little
ripieno – "fill in" part, the
tutti or full parts
risonante – resounding,
ringing
romanza – romance
rotondo – round or full as
regards to tone
rustico – rustic, rural
saltando – in a jumping or
skipping style
salto – a skip
scemando – diminishing in
power of tone
scherzato – playfully
schietto – simple, plain, neat
scordato – out of tune
secco – dry, plain, without
ornament
semplice – simplicity
sereno – serene, tranquil
sforzato – forced, with
emphasis
sforzando – forced, with
emphasis
silenzio – silence, a rest
si piace – at pleasure
si tace – be silent
soave – softly, sweetly
solito – in the same manner

sonabile – sounding, reso-
nant
sonare – to sound, to play
upon
sono – sound
sorda – muffled, veiled
spinato – smooth, level, even
spiccatamente – brightly,
brilliantly
spirituale – spiritual
stabile – firm, steady
staccare – to make staccato
stentato – forced, empha-
sized
steso – extended, stesso–
same
strepitoso – very loud, noisy
stretta – taken in quicker
time
stretto – close, contracted,
drawn together
strisciando – sliding
smoothly from one note
to another
suavemente – with sweet-
ness and delicacy
svegliato – lively, briskly
taci – be silent
tace – be silent
tempestoso – tempestuously
tempo comodo – in conve-
nient time

tempo di ballo – in dance rhythm
tempo di marcia – in march time
tempo di valse – in waltz time

tempo giusto – in exact time
tumultuoso – agitated, tumultuous
uguale – equal, like
variamente – varied, freely
vigoroso –vigorously

(B) Names of Musical Instruments

English	Abbr.	Italian	French	German
Piccolo	Picc.	Flauto Piccolo (or Ottavino)	Petite Flute	Kleine Flote
Flute	Fl.	Flauto	Flute	Flote
Oboe	Ob.	Oboe	Hautbois	Oboe or Hoboe
English Horn	E.H.	Corno Inglese	Cor Anglais	Englisches Horn
Clarinet	Clar.	Clarinetto	Clarinette	Klarinette
Bass Clarinet	B.Clar.	Clarinetto Basso	Clarinette Basse	Bassklarinette
Bassoon	Bsn.	Fagotto	Basson	Fagott
Contra Bassoon	C. Bsn.	Contrafagotto	Contre-basson	Kontrafagott
Horn	Hn.	Corno	Cor	Horn
Trumpet	Tpt.	Tromba	Trompette	Trompete
Trombone	Trb.	Trombone	Trombone	Posaune
Tuba	Tb.	Tuba	Tuba	Tuba or Basstuba
Timpani	Timp.	Timpani	Timbales	Pauken
Bass Drum	B.D.	Gran Cassa	Grosse Caisse	Grosse Trommel
Snare Drum or Side Drum	S.D.	Tamburo (Militare)	Tambour (Militaire)	Kleine Trommel
Cymbals	Cym.	Piatti	Cymbales	Becken
Triangle	Tr.	Triangolo	Triangle	Triangel

English	Abbr.	Italian	French	German
Glockenspiel	Glock.	Campanelli	Jeu. de Timbres (or Carillon)	Glocken-spiel
Violin	Vl.	Violino	Violon	Violine
Viola	Vla.	Viola	Alto	Bratsche
Violoncello or Cello	Vc.	Violoncello	Violoncelle	Violoncell
Double Bass or String Bass	D.B.	Contrabasso	Contre Basse	Kontrabass

(C) Form in Music

In General

Beyond considerations of melody, rhythm, and harmony in music is the concept of musical form or structure. Form is the way in which a composer organizes what he has to say in a manner which will make it possible for the listener to understand the music, especially if the composition is longer than a minute or so.

Musical form depends upon unity and variety: unity to impress the listener that the music is organized, meaningful sound rather than nonsense; and variety, to sustain interest, to relieve boredom, and to provide contrast.

Unity is achieved by repetition, either exact or modified, of a musical idea. Variety comes about by using new material, or by using the original musical idea in such a transformed manner that the transformation itself gives contrast.

Repetition is two-fold: (1) the repetition of a short motive used in such a way as to build phrases, and (2) repetition of the phrases themselves, or of larger parts of the composition. *The motive.* As used by most significant composers, the motive is a short, meaningful melodic fragment which contains, in essence, the musical idea of the whole composition.

Qualities of a motive. The significant aspects or qualities of the motive, and the way in which these qualities may be varied include the following:

1. The notes themselves. They may be varied by changing the order (a-b-c-d becomes b-a-c-d, b-a-d-c, etc.); by extension (a-b-c-d becomes a-b-b-c-d, a-a-b-c-d-d, etc.); by contraction (a-b-c-d becomes a-b-c, b-c-d, a-b-d, etc.); by extension and contraction (a-b-c-d becomes a-b-b-c, etc.)

2. The intervals. These include the melodic intervals making up the motive, and in addition the interval from the lowest to the highest note and the interval from the first to the last note. These may be varied by changing the quality (c-g, a perfect fifth, becomes c-g flat, a diminished fifth); by changing the size (c-f, a fourth, becomes c-a, a sixth); or by inversion (c-e becomes e-c). If successive changes are used, systematically increasing or decreasing the interval, but always in the same direction, one can speak of "developing" the interval.

3. The melodic curve. In general, a motive may go up, down, or zig-zag. The direction of the melodic curve may be changed by contrary motion (c-e-g-a becomes g-e-c-d) or by the use of retrograde (reverse) motion (c-e-g-a becomes a-g-e-c).

4. The rhythm. This may be changed by augmentation (all notes in twice the original value, or in some other multiple of it); by diminution (all notes in half, or some other fraction, of the value); by shifting the rhythm pattern in such a way as to reverse the positions of accents; by introducing, or omitting, or extending, or shortening the upbeat.

5. Transposition. The motive, or any of its variations, may appear on any degree, or in any key, that is appropriate to the musical purpose.

Phrases may be built on a succession of variants of the motive. These may overlap, and can, of course, be adapted to any immediate necessity, such as the establishment of a cadence, the chord of the moment, or the requirements of imitation.

Phrase. The phrase is a unit of musical structure, roughly corresponding to the length of the breath, or to that of a line of poetry. Normally, the phrase extends through four measures of moderate tempo, but three-measure phrases and five-measure phrases are not infrequent. The phrase ends in a cadence of greater or less finality, depending upon the function of the phrase in the composition as a whole.

Period. The period is made up of two phrases, the antecedent (first) phrase and the consequent phrase. Frequently the first phrase ends in a half cadence and the second in a perfect cadence, but this feature depends on the musical purpose. If the two phrases begin alike, the period is in parallel construction. Structures of the same type, but larger, such as the double period and the period of three phrases, are met with occasionally.

Chain of phrases. Frequently a larger part is built up, not in period structure, but in a more or less loosely organized chain of phrases, which may be separated by cadences, but which frequently show *elision* of the cadence (the last chord of one phrase is used as the first chord of the next) or *dissolution* of the cadence (the harmonic progression is characteristic of a cadence, but the rhythm is not interrupted; the cadential measure is broken up into notes of small value). Phrase chains are frequent in the expositions of sonatas by Haydn and Mozart.

Musical Forms

The combination of the various elements of music into understandable and interesting structures constitutes musical form. Most music falls into types, or musical forms, which resemble each other sufficiently to have acquired names; and a knowledge of these names and of the structural patterns they represent is essential to well-rounded musicianship.

However, it must be understood that these are forms and not formulas. While from the standpoint of theoretical analysis it would be convenient if musical compositions were all in clearly defined categories, with no overlapping, composers have never cooperated. A genuine composer uses set forms only to the extent consistent with his own purposes, and has no hesitation in modifying existing forms or creating new ones.

A convenient broad classification of forms separates them into two groups: homophonic (one-voiced) forms and polyphonic (many-voiced) forms. In homophonic forms, the music is set forth in divisions called parts, and the texture usually consists of one prominent voice, the melody, which is accompanied by other voices which are subordinate to the melody. The usual plan is melody, bass, and one or more voices as "filler." Polyphonic forms, on the other hand, have a degree of independence in the voices, no one of which is consistently more important than any other. The linear divisions, or sections, are less clearly defined, and the musical meaning is made apparent by the interplay of the various voices. The differences will become more apparent to the student if he or she analyzes various examples, and if he or she becomes familiar with the list of forms which concludes this chapter.

Homophonic forms. Homophonic forms are classified into

small forms and large forms, on the basis of relative complexity of structure, rather than on absolute length.

Small forms are built up of parts, which are simple in structure (period, double-period, or phrase-chain.) These are arranged in two ways: the two-part song form (A, B) and the three-part song form (A, B, A). The letters are applied to the parts for identification, so that a two-part form consists of one idea which ends away from the tonic and a second, different part which returns to the tonic and so achieves balance. In three-part form, the first part (A) is followed by a contrasting part (B) with a return to the original idea. The (A) part of a three-part form either ends in the tonic, or leads, in its restatement, to a coda which establishes the original key and brings the composition to a close.

In the large forms, the individual parts are themselves small forms. Accordingly, the large form represents two levels of organization. For example, a rondo my have the form A-B-A-C-A-D-A, in which A is three-part form, a-b-a, and the other parts may be similarly complex.

The most important small forms are these:

> Two-part song form, A-B
> Three-part song form, A-B-A
> Minuet or scherzo, A-B (or A-B-A); C-D (or C-D-C); A-B
>   (or A-B-A)

The most important large forms are

> Variation forms (A, A^1, A^2, etc., where A is complex)
> Rondos: small rondo A-B-A
>   old (or second) rondo A-B-A-C-A-D-A
>   new (or third) rondo A-B-A-C-A-B-A
> Sonata-allegro: exposition-development-recapitulation.

The sonata and the suite are forms made up of two or more

(typically four) movements, each of which may be a large form.

All the forms mentioned are discussed in greater detail in the list of terms to follow.

Polyphonic forms. Counterpoint is the art of composing music by combining melodies. The music which results is known as polyphonic (many-voiced) music. This technique of composition was used almost exclusively from the time of the earliest music for more than one voice (shortly before 1000 A.D.) to the middle of the 18th century. After a period of emphasis on harmonic technique in the late 18th and the entire l9th centuries, counterpoint is again in the 20th century characteristic of the work of many important composers.

Certain musical structures have emerged which are called polyphonic, or contrapuntal forms. These include the canon, the motet, the madrigal, and the mass, as vocal forms, and the chorale prelude, the fugue, and the suite (in the sense of the classical set of dances of Bach's time) for instruments. Canons are also written for instruments. Occasionally a fugue is used as a movement in a sonata or a symphony, for example the finale of Mozart's C major (Jupiter) Symphony. Each of the forms listed in this paragraph is discussed in some detail in the list which follows.

List of Terms

This list contains a brief discussion or identification of many of the terms used in connection with musical form. For more complete information, standard reference works should be consulted.

Allemande: A classic dance in $\frac{4}{4}$ measure, moderately fast, usually with an eighth-note upbeat. See Suite (1). The name means "German dance."

Anthem: A piece of sacred choral music used in the service of Protestant churches, sung by the choir, rather than by the congregation. It is usually accompanied by the organ and may contain solos by one or more voices, and concerted passages for solo voices (duets, trios, or quartets).

Aria: A solo song, occurring in an opera, oratorio, or cantata, which develops a dramatic, lyric, or emotional high point in the work. Unlike the recitatives it does not usually advance the action of the plot. In the 18th century, the aria normally consisted of an orchestral introduction, a long section for the accompanied solo voices a section in contrasting key and style, and a reprise of the entire first section. For this reason, it was frequently called the "da capo" aria. Some composers, including Gluck, Wagner, and Debussy, did not maintain the difference between the aria and the recitative, but used a mixed technique, partaking of both declamation and expressive song.

Arioso: A style of solo song in opera or oratorio, resembling both the recitative and the aria. It maintains the careful treatment of the text characteristic of the recitatives but it is likely to be melodious, and to preserve something of the symmetry and key unity characteristic of the aria. Wagner's music dramas make wide use of the arioso.

Bagatelle: Literally, a trifle. The name was applied by Beethoven and others to short piano pieces, usually in song form.

Ballad, ballade:
   (1) A simple song
   (2) A narrative poem, set to music, such as Schubert's "Erl-King."
   (3) A piano piece, orchestral work, or choral work, which is patterned after the above definition. Chopin's four ballades for the piano are examples.

Basso ostinato: Literally, an obstinate bass. A variation form in which a bass-line of 1, 2, or 4 bars is repeated over and over, with changing harmonies and melodies above. There are a few entire pieces of this sort, but frequently the basso ostinato occurs as one section of a larger work, for example in measures 118 through 128 of the last movement of the first symphony of Brahms.

Cadence: An interruption to the movement of music, usually at the end of a phrase. The interruption is put into effect by one or more of the following devices:
   (1) *Duration:* The final chord of the cadence, or at least the melody note, is comparatively long.
   (2) *Melodic movement:* The final melody note of the cadence is an inactive tone.
   (3) *Metrical position:* The final note of the cadence is usually in a strong metrical position, frequently on the first beat of the measure. However, a reverse may be true, in which case the cadence is called a feminine ending.
   (4) *Chord progression:* The chord progression of the cadence is such as to give the feeling of repose.
Types of cadences: The harmonic element of the cadential effect is so important that cadences are usually classified according to harmonic progression:

(1) *Perfect authentic cadence:* V-I or V7-I, both chords in root position, with the root of I in the highest voice. This is the usual formula for ending a piece, and is often preceded by a I 6-4 chord.

(2) *Perfect plagal cadence:* IV-I, sometimes used independently, but most frequently as the "Amen" sung after the last verse of a hymn.

Perfect cadences are sometimes called "full closes."

(3) *Imperfect cadence:* A weak form of the perfect authentic cadence. The chord progression is V-I or V7-I, but one or the other of the chords is inverted, or the soprano note of the last chord is not the root.

(4) *Half cadence:* A cadence ending on V, or on III of minor keys. Half cadences may also end on other degrees, but not the tonic.

(5) *Deceptive (or interrupted) cadence:* A special kind of half-cadence, in which the listener's ear is prepared for a perfect authentic cadence, but the final chord turns out to be some chord other than the tonic. (Examples: V-VI; V-IV).

Canon: A composition for two or more voice-parts, in which each of the parts in turn presents the identical melody (called the subject) in a way dictated by the first voice, and by the conventions adopted for the canon. The canon is the strictest of the contrapuntal forms using imitation.

Canons are described by the number of voices and the number of subjects. A canon 3 in 1 is a canon for three voices using one subject. A canon 4 in 2 is for four voices, using two subjects.

Canons may also be described by the interval of imitation and by the distance (in time) between the entrance of the subject and the beginning of the imitation. A canon may be written at the octave (fifth, sixth, etc.) after two measures (one beat, four measures, etc.)

A canon which returns to its starting point is a perpetual or infinite canon. A canon which has a definite close is a finite canon.

Imitation may be direct, but may also be in inversion, (or contrary motion), in augmentation, in diminution, or retrograde.

Canons are usually independent, but may be accompanied by one or more voices which do not participate in the imitation.

Cantata: Originally, a piece of music for singing, as contrasted to a piece to be played on instruments (sonata). Now the term usually refers to a sacred or secular work for soloists, chorus, and orchestra, something like a short oratorio or an opera not intended for action. Bach wrote more than 200 cantatas for performance in the Lutheran service before the sermon.

Caprice, capriccio: A fanciful and irregular sort of composition written in free style, resembling the *fantasia.*

Cassation: A name applied by Mozart and others to some serenades, or suites, for various instrumentations, probably intended for outdoor performance.

Chaconne or Passacaglia: A composition consisting of a set of variations derived from a ground bass 4 or 8 measures long, usually in triple meter. Originally dances of Spanish origin, the chaconne and passacaglia have become the framework of some of the finest music of some of the greatest composers, for example: the Chaconne from Bach's D minor partita for violin alone, the Passacaglia in C minor by the same composer, Beethoven's Thirty-two Variations in C minor, Chopin's Berceuse, and the Finale of Brahms' Fourth Symphony. Some theorists make various distinctions between the chaconne and passacaglia as forms, but analysis of the music fails to show any consistent difference.

Chorale: The German hymn developed by Martin Luther. It is of great musical importance because it became the basis of much German music up to the middle of the 18th century, especially in the chorale prelude for organ, and in the cantata. Bach harmonized about 400 of these traditional melodies, and based much of his church music on them.

Chorale Prelude: An elaboration of a chorale melody for the organ, used in the Lutheran service as a prelude to the singing of the chorale by the congregation. Fine examples were composed by Bach and Brahms, among others. The form is also sometimes called chorale elaboration or chorale figuration.

Concerto: A large work for soloist with orchestra, in the form of a sonata or symphony. It ordinarily consists of three movements, the first being in sonata-allegro form with double exposition (a *ritornello* for orchestra and a second statement of the themes by the solo instrument), a slow second movement, and a rapid and brilliant third movement, usually a rondo. Nearly always the first movement has, at the end of the recapitulation, a six-four chord with a fermata, at which point the orchestra stops and the soloist plays an extended brilliant passage called a *cadenza* elaborating on the themes of the movement. Cadenzas may also be introduced at appropriate points in the other movements. Originally, cadenzas were improvised by the soloist, but Beethoven began the practice of writing them out exactly as he wanted them played. Today, the practice of improvising cadenzas has almost died out.

Concerto grosso: A form originating in the late 17th century, in which a small group of solo instruments (the concertino) is set against a larger body of accompanying instruments (the concerto grosso, sometimes called the ripieno). Handel, Torelli, Bach (particularly in the Brandenburg Concertos), and Locatelli were great masters of this form. There has been a revival of interest in the concerto grosso in the 20th century in the work of Bloch and others.

Courante: A classic dance in rapid tempo, usually with $\frac{3}{4}$ or $\frac{6}{4}$ measure, with an upbeat of one quarter-note or three eighth notes. The name means "running dance." See Suite (1).

Descant: (1) A term used after the 12th century to denote any kind of polyphony. (2) In modern usage, a countermelody, usually florid, superimposed above the principal melody of a chorale.

Development: In the sonata allegro, the section between the exposition and the recapitulation, consisting of a working out of fragments of the themes presented in the exposition, frequently using modulation. The development ordinarily ends with a retransition to the principal key, introducing the main theme.

   In the fugue, the section after the exposition. It elaborates the subject by one or more of the following means: modulation, stretto, augmentation, diminution, fragmentary treatment, invertible counterpoint (with one or more counter subjects.)

Divertimento: A type of suite typical of the late 18th century, written for various small instrumental combinations and intended for outdoor performance. There is no real difference between serenade, cassation, and divertimento in this sense. All were for much the same purpose; all have typically more than four movements; and none has the high degree of organization characteristic of the quartet and trio of the period.

Double fugue: A fugue with two subjects. These may be presented in various ways: (1) Subject A and subject B may be introduced together in two voices; (2) Subject B may appear as the first contrapuntal associate of subject A; and (3) The fugue may have a complete exposition of subject A, followed by another exposition displaying the association of the two subjects. Triple fugues are also possible.

Duo, trio, quartet, sextet, etc.: Specific names, depending upon the number of participating musicians, for classical sonatas for instrumental ensembles. Duos or duo sonatas are usually for two string or wind instruments, or for one string and one wind. A duo sonata for piano and another instrument is ordinarily called by such names as a sonata for violin and piano, or for clarinet and piano, or even a sonata for piano with violin accompaniment (this was the title used by Mozart and Beethoven.) In such works all parts are coordinate and of substantially equal importance.

Episode: In a fugal work, an interlude between statements of the subject. An episode may be for the purpose of bringing a section of the work to a close, in which case it is sometimes called a codetta (coda for the final cadence); or it may serve to modulate to a new statement of the subject in a different key; or it may have no other purpose than to provide for formal balance.

Etude: Basically, a piece written for the practice of some particular technical difficulty. As such, the etude is likely to have a repeated figure which contains the technical difficulty occurring throughout the composition. Some etudes are of sufficient musical value to have attained the stature of concert pieces; for example, the Etudes of Chopin and Liszt and the Symphonic Etudes for piano of Schumann.

Exposition: (1) In fugal works, the first section of the work in which the subject is stated by each of the voices in turn, each statement after the first combined with the counter-subject or other appropriate counterpoint, and ending in an episode which leads to a cadence introducing the development. The cadence is frequently weakened by elision or may be dissolved. (See cadence.)

(2) The first large section of a sonata-allegro, in which the main theme and subordinate theme are presented in contrast with each other ending in a cadence in a related key, which ushers in the development.

Fantasia (fantasie, fancy): A name given to various kinds of composition which agree in being free in style, not restricted to any definite form.

The figure: The figure resembles the motive to the extent that it is a short group of notes. It differs from the motive, however, in that it serves only a subsidiary purpose, as an accompaniment.

Fox trot: A term applied to a piece of music usually written in $\frac{4}{4}$ or ¢ meter played by a modern dance band for ballroom dancing.

Fugato: A passage in fugal style appearing in a non-fugal composition. For example, a single variation in a set of variations may be a fugato; a concerted piece or a chorus in an opera or oratorio may be a fugato.

Fughetta: A short fugue.

Fugue: Probably the most important of the techniques of contrapuntal writing. A fugue is a composition, usually for a fixed number of voices, either vocal or instrumental, in which a melodic idea, or subject, is treated by imitation in all the voices, and in which the imitative sections are separated by episodes.

Properly speaking, the fugue is not a form, because no two fugues are alike in structure. The formal aspect of any fugue depends on two factors: (1) the characteristics of the subject itself, whether it is suitable for stretto, or for statement in contrary motion, or can imitate itself in augmentation or diminution, and other similar considerations, and (2) the skill and imagination of the composer. However, some generalizations can be made, which should be verified by the analysis of a number of fugues.

The first section of a fugue, or *exposition*, states the subject by each of the voices in turn, alternating between statements in the tonic and in the dominant. The statements in the dominant are called *answers*. This procedure sets up a basic conflict, which does much to produce the tension necessary to give drive and impetus to the work. As the second and other following voices state the subject or answer, the voices which have already entered proceed in counterpoint. If the counterpoint (or contrapuntal associate) is used consistently, it is called a counter-subject; if it is used invariably it is a second subject, and the fugue is a double fugue. (See double fugue.)

When all the voices are in, an episode, usually derived from the subject, leads to a cadence in a related key. This cadence closes the exposition, and introduces the development, which exploits the capabilities of the subject and its combination with itself and with other material of the exposition in whatever ways the composer thinks appropriate. There may be more than one development section, each exploiting a particular technique.

The final section of the fugue is the recapitulation, which may restate the subject in only one outside voice in the tonic, but which may introduce the subject in each of the voices in turn, in stretto, if feasible, to heighten the excitement, but usually in *repercussion* (that is, the statement of the subject by all voices in a different order of appearance from that of the exposition.)

Galop: A lively dance in $\frac{2}{4}$ measure. Example: Galop from Orpheus in The Underworld, by Offenbach.

Gavotte: A dance consisting of two lively strains in $\frac{4}{4}$ time, usually with an upbeat of two quarter-notes. It sometimes alternates with a musette, which is a gavotte over a drone bass, an imitation of bagpipes.

Gigue (giga): A classic dance in $\frac{6}{8}$ or $\frac{12}{8}$ measure, in rapid tempo. The second part usually begins with the inversion of the main theme. See Suite (1).

Impromptu: A piece in free style, as though improvised. Actually, an impromptu is likely to be a song form or a small rondo in spite of its name.

Intermezzo: An interlude; a piece of instrumental music between the acts of an opera.

Invention: A name used by Bach to describe a set of fifteen keyboard pieces in two parts, written for the training of his sons in composition as well as in performance. They resemble fugues in that they are imitative, but differ in the comparative freedom of their style, in the fact that imitation is normally in the octave in the inventions, and in their smaller size. Many other contrapuntal works by Bach and others, called preludes, duets, and other names, can be considered to be inventions. The three-part "inventions" frequently published together with the two-part inventions were called "symphonies" (sinfonien) by Bach.

Latin American dance forms: Latin American dance music is characterized by the use of a host of unusual percussion instruments each of which has its particular assigned part. Rhythm is therefore the outstanding feature with harmony and melody in the background.

    Rhumba: The rhumba originated in Cuba. The fundamental rhythmic pattern is played by the piano, bass, and bass drum.

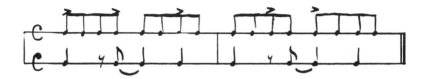

Another variety of rhumba is the *Guaracha* in which the fourth beat of the bar receives two eighth note accents.

Bolero: The Cuban or $\frac{4}{4}$ bolero is entirely different from the original Spanish or $\frac{3}{4}$ bolero. The bolero of today as danced in the modern ballroom is the Cuban variety.

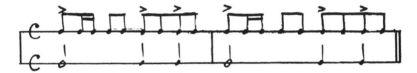

Samba: A characteristic Brazilian dance form with rolling rhythm and a strong feeling of two to the bar.

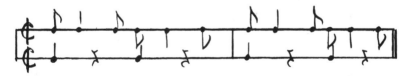

Tango: A widely popular dance from Argentina. Main characteristic is the heavy accent on the fourth beat or after-beat of four.

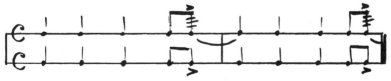

Mambo: A recent addition to the Latin American dance group. An outstanding characteristic is the strong accent on two and four in a two-bar pattern.

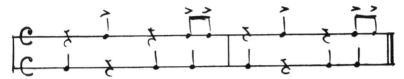

Additional Latin American dance forms in common use are the *Conga, Son, Calypso,* and numerous variants of the principal forms.

Lied: In the narrow sense, a German art-song, as written by Schubert, Schumann, Brahms, Wolf, and others. It is characterized by effective union of the music with the words, not only with respect to the natural accents and speech tune of the language, but also with the mood of the poem. A distinction is made between the strophic lied, which used the same music for each stanza of the poem, and the "through-composed" (durchkomponiert) lied, in which each verse is set differently, a device particularly suited to a poem in which the mood develops or changes from stanza to stanza.

Madrigal: Although the word appears as early as the late 13th century applied to vocal compositions in two or three parts, it refers chiefly to a type of secular polyphonic vocal composition which flourished in Italy and England during the last part of the 16th century and well into the 17th century. Although designed as a sort of vocal chamber music in the home, with one singer to a part, madrigals are commonly sung by choruses today. The fact that instruments were used to supply missing parts or to reinforce weak singers stimulated the use of instrumental music and the eventual development of music for instruments only.

March: A musical composition designed to produce orderliness and spirit in the movement of troops, or to provide music for the accompaniment of processions.

Broadly, marches can be classed as processional or grand marches (with the funeral march as a special variety) and fast marches or quicksteps. Grand marches are in $\frac{4}{4}$ or $\frac{12}{8}$ meter, and in moderate tempo. Fast marches are two beats in the measure, either $\frac{2}{2}$, $\frac{2}{4}$, or $\frac{6}{8}$. American marches, of the kind made famous by Sousa, Goldman, King, Panella, Chambers, Farrar, and others, consist of two repeated strains in the main key, followed by a trio in the key of the subdominant. The trio may consist of a repeated strain, followed by a contrasting break strain, after which the main theme of the trio is repeated, usually with reinforced or brilliant instrumentation. English marches often repeat the first two strains after the trio is played, making the form quite similar to that of a minuet.

Concert marches are written for the sole purpose of being played at concerts. Such marches usually contain features which make them unsuitable for marching.

Mass: The observance of the Eucharist in certain churches. Musically, it consists of the proper, intoned by the priest, and varying in content from day to day throughout the church calendar, and the ordinary, or invariable portion, which may be sung by the choir. When a "mass" by a composer is spoken of, the ordinary is meant. This consists of six parts:

(1) Kyrie eleison (Lord, have mercy upon us)
(2) Gloria (Glory to God in the Highest)
(3) Credo (I believe)
(4) Sanctus (Holy, holy art Thou, Lord God)
(5) Benedictus (Blessed is He that cometh)
(6) Agnus Dei (Lamb of God, who takest away the sins of the world)

Mazurka: A lively Polish dance in $\frac{3}{4}$ or $\frac{3}{8}$ meter, with emphasis on the second or third beat of the measure.

Minuet: A dance popular in Europe from about 1650 to the beginning of the 19th century, particularly valued as it was considered to be the best training in genteel deportment. It was in $\frac{3}{4}$ meter, in moderate tempo. Serious composers used it as an optional dance in the suite (see Suite 1) and later in the symphony, in which use it was displaced eventually by the scherzo. It is normally written as a three-part song form, but may be in two parts. Frequently it has a trio, with da capo to the first minuet.

Motet: A polyphonic choral composition setting Latin religious words other than those of the mass. The great development of the motet was in the 16th century, notably in the work of Palestrina, Lassus, and Victoria, who produced some of the finest music of all time in this form.

Opera: One of the most important of musical forms, uniting at the same time the efforts of the poet (librettist), the actor, the stage-crafter, and the costumer with that of the composer. The musical requirements for performance are for soloists, orchestra, and chorus. Historically, and simultaneously in almost every era, opera has meant a great variety of styles and purposes, from light and even farcical operetta and musical comedy on the one hand to the most profound and moving drama on the other. National schools and individual composers have varied from one extreme to the other in balancing the relative weight of drama and music. Verdi, Wagner, and Mozart are among the most significant composers of opera.

Oratorio: A dramatic work for soloists, chorus, and orchestra, the libretto of which concerns a sacred subject. It differs from opera in the fact that it is not written to be acted on the stage. There is generally more emphasis on the part of the chorus. The best known oratorio is the "Messiah" of Handel, only one of many fine works by that composer. Others are by Mendelssohn, Haydn, Beethoven, and among moderns, Walton and Honegger.

Overture:
   (1) The orchestral introduction to an opera, oratorio, or cantata.
   (2) A piece of keyboard or orchestral music patterned after the overture in the first sense, but intended for independent performance.
   The overture originated as a device to get the attention of the crowd assembled to hear the opera. In the 17th century, two forms, each in three movements, arose: the Italian (fast, slow, fast) and the French (slow, fast, slow).
   In Bach's time overture often meant a suite which began with a slow movement full of dotted rhythms, like that of the

French overture, but which had additional movements in the form of dances.

The form of the modern overture is likely to be that of the sonata-allegro, but there are many overtures which are only medleys or potpourris of tunes. Some of these are associated with light operas.

Partita: Another name for suite (1), but usually referring to a rather elaborate suite, introduced by a movement not in dance rhythm, such as a prelude, overture, sinfonia, toccata, fantasie, or preambulum, introducing extra movements, such as gavottes, minuets, bourrees, airs, or polonaises, and frequently having doubles for one or more of the movements. The best-known partitas are a set of six by J. S. Bach.

Passacaglia: See *chaconne.*

Passage: When a motive is used sequentially in a florid manner, or dissolves into a scale or apreggio figure for the sake of brilliance, it is known as a passage.

Passepied: A rapid dance, three beats to the measure, with an upbeat of one beat. It was occasionally used as an optional movement in a suite.

Passion: A piece of sacred music, resembling an oratorio, based on the last events in the life of Christ, and derived from the custom in some churches of devoting four days of Holy Week to the reading of the story of Christ's life from the various gospels. Traditionally, in a musical passion, the story is carried forward by a tenor, "the Evangelist" who acts as narrator and who sings mostly in recitative. The part of Christ is given to a bass, accompanied by strings. Other parts sometimes appear for Peter, Pilate, Judas, and various other characters. The chorus is used for heightened moments of feeling, and for reflective passages. The greatest passions were written by Bach and Schütz.

Polka: A lively Bohemian or Polish dance in $\frac{2}{4}$ meter, with the first three eighth-notes accented, and the fourth unaccented. Another form similar to the Polka is the *Schottische*.

Polonaise: A stately Polish dance in $\frac{3}{4}$ meter, with each of the beats normally divided into two eighth-notes, but with the last half of the first beat divided into two sixteenth notes. There is an important secondary stress on the second beat.

Prelude:
    (1) A piece played as an introduction to another, as a prelude and fugue.
    (2) Any short piece in rather free style is likely to be called a prelude by its composer, for example the preludes of Chopin and Rachmaninoff.

Recapitulation:
    (1) In fugues, the section which prepares for the close of the work. The recapitulation may be elaborate enough to contain a statement of the fugue subject in the main key by each of the voices; or it may be limited to a single statement, in the bass or soprano. In any case, the recapitulation is usually followed by an extension, which is called a coda, leading to the final cadence.
    (2) In the sonata form, the section which follows the de-

velopment and brings the movement to a close. It stands in the main key, and presents both the main theme and the subordinate theme. It differs from the exposition in that the two themes are almost always in the same key. Aesthetically, this procedure serves the purpose of reconciling the two themes, after building most of the movement on the conflict between them. The recapitulation is preceded by a retransition, and usually followed by a coda.

Recitative: In the opera, oratorio, and other extended dramatic works a style of writing which imitates the effects of spoken language, without much regard to melody or to rhythmic regularity. It is used for narrative, dialogue, or for situations unsuited to lyric expression. (See aria.) In light opera, recitative is supplanted, for the most part, by spoken dialogue.

Retransition: A transition, bridge passage, or extension which occurs as the final event in a development section. Its purpose is to prepare for the reentry of the main theme in the principal key. In classic works, this is frequently accomplished by dwelling on the dominant of the key.

Rigaudon: An old dance in duple meter originating in southern France and occasionally used in the suite, or as an independent number.

Rondo: A large form made by the contrast of a main theme with one or more contrasting subordinate themes. The theme (A) is likely to be a small song-form, or at least a chain of phrases or double period. Three types are distinguished:

The small rondo (first rondo) in which there is only one digression. The digression may be a lyric theme, but is more likely to be a shifting, passage-like development of some fragment of the main theme. This is followed by a return to the original theme, this time, however, in more elaborate treatment and followed by a coda. The tempo of the small rondo is nearly always slow: andante or adagio. The slow movement of many sonatas and symphonies are in this form.

The old (or second) rondo, which is a rapid piece, in which there are two or more different digressions, last of which is likely to be in a somewhat remote key.

The new (or third) rondo, also rapid in tempo. It differs from the second rondo in having a return to the first digression (A-B-A-C-A-B-A). This practice makes for greater unity.

Second and third rondos are often found as independent pieces, and are also quite frequent as the final movements of sonatas, symphonies, and similar works.

Sarabande: A classic dance of Spanish origin in slow $\frac{3}{4}$ or $\frac{3}{2}$ measure, with the second beat accented or lengthened. See Suite (1).

Scherzo: The term is the Italian word for joke, and this is typical of many specimens of the musical scherzo. Ordinarily, a scherzo is a movement in sonatas, symphonies, quartets, and the like, which replaces the minuet. Like the minuet, it is in triple meter, but it is faster. Haydn appears to be the first to have made the substitution, but Beethoven was the first to use it rather consistently. The name is also applied to separate works similar in form (which is identical to that of the minuet) but having tragic or dramatic implications, such as the scherzi of Chopin and Brahms for piano.

Serenade: See *cassation, divertimento.*

Sonata-allegro: A large form used as the first movement of sonatas, symphonies, quartets, and the like, and separately as the overture.

The form depends for its interest on the use of two themes which are first stated in contrast, then developed, then finally reconciled. The main theme and subordinate theme are likely to be different in style–one heroic, the other lyric or elegaic; they are in contrasting keys or regions (tonic — dominant, or minor tonic — relative major). Structurally, they may be extended periods, or phrase-chains. There is usually a bridge passage leading from the main theme to the subordinate theme, and another from the subordinate theme to the cadence which ends the exposition.

The development section uses all sorts of techniques to explore or work out the two, themes or fragments of them separately and in relation to each other. (See development.)

The recapitulation finally restates the themes but now in the same key. The movement, at least in the larger examples, is likely to have an extension at the end called a coda.

Sonata: A large form in several movements, each of which is also likely to be a large form. The same form is used for duos, trios, quartets, and other chamber music works; for symphonies, which are essentially sonatas for orchestra; and for concerti, which are sonatas for solo instrument with orchestra.

The typical large sonata is in four movements, the first a sonata-allegro, the second a small rondo or other slow movement in a related key, the third a minuet or scherzo in still another related key, and the final movement a rondo or another sonata-allegro in the main key. Works in three movements usually omit the minuet. A theme with variations may be substituted for any of the four movements.

Sonatina: A small sonata with less elaborate treatment of thematic material than in the sonata.

Song: In its broadest sense, vocal music, uniting words with melody. A distinction is made between folk-song, which is the work of unschooled composers, handed down and modified by tradition, and art-song, which is music composed essentially for performance by skilled singers. (See Lied.)

Stretto: A type of imitation, frequent in fugues, in which the follower begins the imitation while the first statement is in progress. Stretto serves to produce increased tension or excitement.

Suite:
  (1) A set of dances, basically consisting of Allemande, Courante, Sarabande, and Gigue, but frequently having an introductory movement, and interpolating other dances, such as Gavotte, Minuet, or Passepied, and even pieces called "Air." This was the suite as written by Bach, Handel, and their predecessors and contemporaries.
  (2) A set of pieces for open-air performance. (See *Serenade, Divertimento, Cassation.*)
  (3) A set of pieces made up of theatrical music, such as Bizet's "Arlesienne Suites," or of music around a central theme, such as Grieg's "From Holbergs Time," or of assorted pieces, more or less related by occasion, key, or theme.

Symphonic Poem (Tone Poem, Tondichtung): A romantic variant of the symphony, breaking down the separation into movements, and incorporating elements of descriptive music (imitating actual extra-musical sounds) or program music

(music which seeks to tell a story). Good examples, besides those of Liszt, are symphonic poems by Richard Strauss and Smetana.

Symphony: As used today, the name refers to an extended sonata for full orchestra. It originated in the middle of the 18th century with Sammartini, Stamitz and Monn; was developed and more or less crystallized into classic form by Haydn, Mozart, and Beethoven; and has been the subject of experimentation and development by almost every significant romantic and modern composer. A great part of the programs of symphony orchestras is made up of symphonies, symphonic poem, concerti, and overtures, all of which are closely related, and all of which are discussed separately in the present list.

Tarantelle, tarantella: A rapid Italian dance in $\frac{6}{8}$ meter, so called either because it originated in the region of Taranto, or because the dance was long regarded as a specific remedy for the bite of the tarantula.

Toccata: Usually, a piece written to display rapidity of execution on a keyboard instrument. It is written in rhapsodic style, and resembles the fantasia. The harpsichord toccatas of Bach, however, are extended pieces alternating sections of brilliant passage-work with slow lyrical sections and with elaborate fugues.

Tone Poem: See *Symphonic Poem.*

Trio:

    (1) A sonata for three instruments, such as a string trio for violin, viola, and cello; a piano trio for piano, violin,

and cello; or a woodwind trio for oboe, clarinet, and bassoon. The possibilities of combination are almost limitless.

(2) The second large division of a minuet, scherzo, or march, after which the first part is repeated. It is called a trio because, as introduced by Lully in the 17th century this part was set for three instruments, two oboes and a bassoon, by way of contrast to the full orchestra used in the first part.

Variation forms: Variation forms (sets of variations, theme and variations, etc.) are pieces of music constructed by presenting the same musical idea in several successive treatments, preserving the outlines of the original idea. Two main types may be observed:

(1) The ground-bass variations, in which the unifying element is a repeated bass line. This type is exemplified by the basso ostinato, the chaconne, and the passacaglia.

(2) The theme with variations, in which a melody is presented in many transformations. Some of these may be cast in other forms, such as a minuet, a cannon, a waltz, or a march. A common device is the "division variations" in which the theme is broken up first into eighth-notes, then into triplets, then into sixteenths, and so on. There may be variations in the minor, slow variations, and so on, limited only by the inventiveness of the composer.

Variation forms have been the vehicle of some of the noblest musical communication, as witnessed by the Goldberg Variations of Bach, the Eroica and Diabelli variations of Beethoven, and the variations of Schumann and Brahms. Also, variations have produced some inferior music.

Waltz: A dance in triple meter which developed from a German peasant dance, the Ländler. It arose in the last years of the 18th century; and in the first half of the 19th century a specialized type, the "Viennese" waltz, in the hands of Josef Lanner and the Strauss family, reached a tremendous vogue. It is characterized by one chord (and one real pulse) in the bar, which appears as a bass note with chord groups on the second and third quarter notes. The second quarter note of the accompaniment is anticipated a trifle in performance.

The waltz is still popular as a dance, although the steps have changed, and for modern dancing the waltz is played in more moderate tempo.

The form of the Viennese waltz consists of a slow introduction, perhaps anticipating the dance tunes to follow, then a series of four or five separate waltzes, each of two strains, with trio, and a da capo, and finally concluding in an extended coda which recapitulates the set of waltzes and ends with a whirlwind finish of some sort.

(D) Media

One consideration of great importance in the study of music is the knowledge of the media of performance; that is, the means available and customary for the translation of the intent of composers into sound.

It is conjectured that the earliest music was performed with no resources other than those of the human body. The voice could give forth melody, and the rhythm of either melody or the dance could be reinforced by clapping the hands, stamping the feet, or making outcries.

Today, we have a great variety of musical instruments, which in a sense extend the possibilities of the singing voice in making musical sound. Some can produce sounds which are louder, wider in range, and of different tone color. Others can make rhythmic sounds that are more forceful than handclaps or stamping of the feet. These can be combined in a variety of ways, either with other instruments, or with the human voice, which remains one of the most important media for producing music.

Three factors are essential to a musical experience: a composition to be performed, a medium of performance, and a listener. This appendix lists a number of the most common examples of the second factor, the medium of performance.

Vocal Media

The solo voice. The single unaccompanied individual voice is used for a number of musical purposes. Rarely, a professional singer may include a song without accompaniment on a recital; but much more frequent examples are the intonation of liturgical chants by the priest, or the informal singing of familiar songs.

The accompanied solo voice. Most frequently, the solo voice is accompanied by a single keyboard instrument–the piano, the organ, or the harpsichord. Plectrum instruments, such as the guitar, the banjo, and the lute, are also often used for accompanying singing by individuals.

Many songs are also sung to the accompaniment of orchestra, ranging from the popular singer who sings the latest song hit with a combo or dance band, to performance with symphony orchestra or the singing of arias in opera or oratorio.

Ensembles. Much vocal music in parts is performed by small groups, one or two singers to each part. Examples of this practice include the barber-shop quartet, the madrigal group, and concerted numbers in operas and similar works, such as the sextet from Lucia di Lamrermoor. Vocal ensembles are sometimes accompanied, sometimes not.

Choruses and choirs. Much music is performed by large groups of singers, organized into sections according to the range of the voices. A distinction is made between the choir, which normally performs religious music, and chorus, which sings secular music, although this is a difference in repertoire rather than in medium. A choir which sings without accompaniment is called an "a cappella" choir (a choir which sings in the style of the chapel).

A further distinction is made among mixed groups, using both women and men, or boys and men, which are organized into sopranos, altos, tenors, and basses, with further subdivision of each voice part possible; men's choruses or choirs, which contain only tenors and basses, usually subdivided; women's choruses or choirs, which contain only sopranos and altos, usually subdivided; and choirs and choruses of unchanged voices, or children's voices.

The choir or chorus may sing unaccompanied, or may be accompanied by organ, piano, or orchestra.

Instrumental Media

Instrumental solos:

(1) *One instrument alone.* Obviously, the instruments most suited for solo performance are those which have the possibility of simultaneously producing melody and harmony, of which the keyboard instruments are the most versatile. However, there exists a considerable literature of works for violin alone, for cello alone, and even for flute alone, which are to be met with in public performance now and then.

(2) *Solo instrument with keyboard accompaniment.* There is a large field of music in this category. Properly speaking, sonatas for violin and piano, cello and piano should be excluded from this category, as the parts are equal in importance and such works should be considered as chamber music or ensemble literature. However, there is a vast literature of shorter pieces for almost every instrument, accompanied with piano or organ. Even concerti can be performed in this fashion, as piano reductions of the orchestral scores are readily available.

(3) *Solo instrument with orchestra accompaniment.* The most important examples in this category are concerti for various instruments. The solo instruments most frequently employed are piano, violin, cello, flute, viola, organ, clarinet, horn, oboe, bassoon, saxophone, and trumpet in about that order of frequency. There are even concerti for doublebass, tuba, and timpani. Besides concerti, many shorter pieces have been written to display the technical agility and musicianship of solo performers.

(4) *Solo instruments with band accompaniment.* There is a large literature of music for wind instruments with band accompaniment, much of it in the nature of empty display pieces. However, band arrangements of some concerto accompaniments have been made, and are quite effective. It is to be hoped that composers will come to recognize the importance of writing music for this medium.

Ensembles. An instrumental ensemble is a small group of instruments with one player to a part. There is a wide variety of such ensembles, some of the more important of which are discussed here.

(1) *The string-quartet.* By far the most important ensemble for the performance of classical chamber music is the string quartet, consisting of two violins, a viola, and a violoncello. The advantages are wide range, great flexibility and agility, and homogeneity of sound. This music is not intended for public performance, although it is often presented quite effectively in small halls. The string quartets of Haydn, Beethoven, Mozart, Brahms, and others are among the finest musical compositions for any medium.

(2) *Other classical ensembles.* The most important are simply listed.

   a. The duo: two like instruments; violin and cello; viola and cello; flute and cello; oboe and bassoon. Other combinations also occur.

   b. The trio: two violins and cello; violin, viola, and cello; piano, violin, and cello (the piano trio); piano, clarinet, and cello; piano, violin, and horn; etc.

   c. The piano quartet: piano, violin, viola, and cello; piano and any three instruments.

   d. Quintets: string quartet with one additional viola or cello (string quintets); string quartet with piano, clarinet, horn, flute, oboe, etc. (piano quintet, clarinet quintet, etc.). Other combinations of five instruments can occur.

   e. Larger ensembles: sextets, septets, octets, and the like, employing a variety of instrumentations; the chamber orchestra, which amounts to a small symphony orchestra of limited instrumentation.

Orchestra. The standard orchestra of today is the symphony orchestra, an aggregation of 60 to 100 players divided into choirs or sections by types of instrument, as strings, woodwinds, brasses, and percussion. The number actually playing depends upon the work being played. The number of performers is substantially reduced for symphonies by Mozart and Haydn, for example, and the number of wind and percussion players used depends on the requirements of the composer. It is standard practice not to maintain regular chairs in the orchestra for instruments seldom used. When works requiring such instruments are programmed, players are hired for the occasion only. Other types of orchestras existing for special purposes include:

(1) *The theater orchestra.* A smaller orchestra, in which the absence of certain instruments is compensated for by cross-cueing so the missing parts can be played by other instruments. Special types of theater orchestra include the opera orchestra, the studio orchestra (for radio or television broadcast, or to supply background music for motion pictures), and the salon orchestra, which specializes in light music for formal dinners, large scale entertainments, and so on.

(2) *The string orchestra.* An orchestra which specializes in music for strings only, or for one solo instrument with strings.

Band.

(1) Originally, a group of musicians performing together, even including vocalists.

(2) A dance orchestra.

(3) In general present usage, a band is an organization of instrumentalists for the performance of music, excluding stringed instruments. Several sorts are distinguished:

    a. Military band. A band of comparatively small size used for military purposes, for example, to accompany the marching of troops, to officiate at honors and ceremonies, and to provide entertainment at military functions.

    b. Brass band. A type of band very popular in England made up only of brass instruments and percussion.

    c. Symphonic or Concert Band. A large band emphasizing woodwind instruments and striving in performance for standards of musicianship comparable to those of symphony orchestras. Unfortunately, the repertoire is not yet comparable, consisting for the present chiefly of arrangements and of original works composers who are as yet unfamiliar with the capabilities of the band as a musical medium.

Dance orchestras and combos. The dance orchestra may be either functional (for dancing) or of the concert type. It may be of any size ranging from just three instruments to a large orchestra, the only "permanent" part being a rhythm section. A rhythm section usually contains a piano and/or a guitar, a string bass, and drums. Usually when the dance orchestra is small and does not possess "sections" it is referred to as a *combo*. A combo may contain just rhythm instruments or in addition, various combinations of wind instruments.

The instrumentation of commonly used dance orchestras follows:

(1) *The full dance orchestra:* five saxophones, two altos, two tenors, one baritone, each doubling on clarinet or other woodwind instrument; six or eight brass instruments divided evenly between trumpets and trombones; the four man rhythm section.

(2) *The "stock" dance orchestra:* three or four saxophones; three or four brass instruments; the four man rhythm section.

(3) *The small tenor band:* three tenor saxophones; one trumpet; piano, string bass, and drums.

(4) *The "Dixieland Band":* one trumpet; one clarinet; one trombone; one tenor saxophone (optional); rhythm.

Other Media

To conclude, a few specialized types of performance groups are included for the sake of completeness.

Consort. An old English name (16th and 17th centuries) for a group of instruments playing together. If all instruments were of one kind (viols or recorders, for example) the group was known as a "whole consort." If string and wind instruments were both represented, the group was "broken consort." The consort represents an early stage in the development of the orchestra and of chamber music.

Fanfare.
    (1) A short, lively, loud piece for trumpets, sometimes with kettledrums or parade drums; or a similar piece involving other brass instruments. Fanfares are used to direct attention to the entrance of an important personage, or to a display, show, or the like.
    (2) In French usage, the word refers to a brass band. A band using woodwinds and brasses is called a "harmonie."

Fife, Drum, and Bugle Corps. An organization for the performance of field music, that is, marches, fanfares, and the kind of military music which was once developed and used for signaling purposes and for the evolutions of troops. It survives principally in display organizations.

(E) Music Copying

The following section has been prepared with the view of helping the student who is not already an expert copyist to set down his musical ideas in such a way as to be legible.

Pen

There is nothing better than a good, light, well-balanced old-fashioned straight pen, with a cork grip of comfortable size. The point used depends on the size of the notes required. For score work and for march-size paper, a fine point must be used; for parts of larger size, a coarser point is required. Stub points are good. Whether a stiff or a flexible point is used is largely a matter of individual preference. There are special fountain pens for writing music manuscript which are excellent when properly used. They should never be filled with India ink, unless emptied immediately after use, because of clogging.

Always write with a clean point. Keep a small dish of water handy, dip the point and wipe it off with a soft cloth occasionally. When new the point should be "smoked" by holding over a small flame, such as a burning match, for a second or two. This will permit the ink to adhere more readily and improve the feeding. Always let the ink dry; do not use a blotter.

Paper

Choose a paper which does not absorb ink so rapidly as to cause spreading and blurring of the notes, and one which erases well. Unless there is some special restriction for size (march folder, for example), choose for parts a relatively large size, with the staves spaced widely enough to get in added lines above or below the staff without crowding.

Layout

In laying out the job, care should be taken to place the notes evenly, avoiding crowding at the ends of the lines. This may be done by either of two methods: (1) ruling the bar lines ahead of time, so that the staff is divided regularly into 4, 5, 6, or more bars, accommodating the length of bar used to the measures with the most notes, or (2) laying out the noteheads for the measure with the most notes first, then ruling the bar line after the measure. With the second method, care must be taken to adjust the last two or three bars so that they come out even.

Much time can be saved in rehearsal if a means is provided to find the proper place to start again, if the piece must be stopped to work out a difficult passage, or to get a fresh start in reading. Three methods are used: (1) rehearsal letters at significant points, (2) measure numbers at regular intervals such as 10, 20, and so on, and (3) measure numbers in the margins. The last method is probably the best, as the numbers do not interfere with reading the music. The score, in case the third method is used, should have every bar numbered in sequence.

Procedure for Making Notes, etc.

The accompanying examples outline an orderly procedure for making the most frequent notes, rests, clefs, and other symbols. In general, write from left to right. Stem, measure bars, and other vertical lines should be comparatively light, while beams, flags, and noteheads should be heavy. Be particularly careful to make all symbols which require the performer to find a new place in the music (segno, repeat marks, etc.) quite bold, so that they will catch the eye.

Class Exercises

Since the class exercise is not for permanent record, it should be written with pencil. The first considerations are legibility and speed. In particular, avoid making large black noteheads; time spent in grinding out such heads had better be spent on working more exercises, or checking the ones already written. If necessary, make all open noteheads with two strokes. This practice centers the notehead on the intended line or space, and avoids the egg shape which a ring is likely to degenerate into if made too rapidly. Indicate heads for quarter notes, eighth notes, and the like by a single heavy stroke, at an angle, not quite connected to the stem.

Music Copying in General

Stems go up for the notes on the lower half of the staff, and are always placed to the right of the notehead. Stems go down and are placed to the left for notes on the upper half of the staff. The stem for the note on the middle line may go either way but tends to go up and be placed to the right of the notehead.

When two parts are written on one staff, the stems for the upper part all go up, the stems for the lower part all go down regardless of the position of the notehead on the staff. Unisons in half notes or smaller are indicated by one note head with two stems, one going up, the other down. Whole notes as unisons are written interlocked.

When writing seconds, the upper note is placed to the right.

Flags or hooks are always attached to the right side of the stem, whether it is up or down.

Beams are used with two or more notes of similar duration, (except in vocal music when the notes are for separate words or syllables).

Rests are made just as they appear in print except for the quarter rest, which has several forms.

Clefs are more difficult and must be practiced with care. (Never precede a clef sign with a bar line. Only when more than one staff is involved, as in piano music, is this done and then it is used as a brace or bracket.)

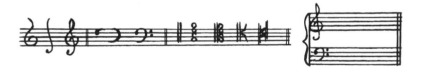

Accidentals and Key Signatures

A Complete Signature

In music written on more than one staff such as piano music, the notes are always written directly under each other in such a way that a vertical line would fall at the same point in the measure in each part.

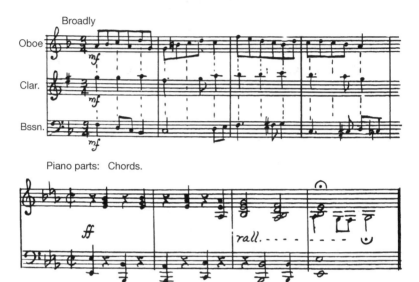

(F) Conducting for Instrumentalists

There are many ties between the conductor and the instrumentalist. The degree to which these ties are felt determines the quality of performance.

The dynamic level and the style or character of the music to be performed will determine the motions of the conductor, but the beat placement (time-beating) will remain basically the same.

The area normally used for time beating is an imaginary square with the top about eye level and the bottom about even with the waist and equidistant to the left and right. If a baton is used, the size of the square will be somewhat larger.

The *down beat* is a vertical movement directly in front of the body going from the upper to the lower part of the square then reversing direction to form the *ictus*. The ictus is the exact place of execution.

The down beat is basically the same for any type of measure. This movement from top to bottom will be referred to as the centerline of the square. (Fig. 1)

The *up beat*, or last beat of the measure, is made by moving from the upper right portion of the square down a slight slant to a spot about one third of the way down the centerline, then changing direction upward to where the movement for the downbeat begins. The change of direction will again provide the ictus for the beat. (Fig. 2)

Now adjust the direction taken after making the ictus for the downbeat to travel to where the upbeat began. This forms the two-beat measure. (Fig. 3)

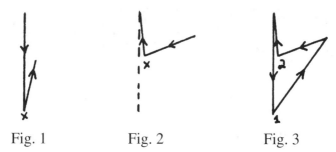

Fig. 1   Fig. 2   Fig. 3

The first beat lasts from the ictus of one to the ictus of two. The second beat lasts from the ictus of two to the ictus of one. The distance the hand travels between beats should be approximately the same to facilitate keeping a steady tempo.

The beat to the right is used for the second beat in $\frac{3}{4}$ and the third beat in $\frac{4}{4}$. To make the beat to the right start a little to the left of center, and move downward almost to the lower right corner of the square, reversing direction there to make the ictus and proceeding to where we began to form the up beat. (Fig. 4)

Adjust the direction of the down beat, after the ictus, to join to the beginning of the beat to the right. Add the up beat and the three beat measure is formed. (Fig. 5)

Fig. 4   Fig. 5

The only other type of beat is the *beat to the left*. This is the Two in a four beat measure. To make the beat to the left, begin on the center line about one third from the bottom of the square and move almost to the lower left corner, then reverse direction, to form the ictus, and proceed to where we began to form the beat to the right. (Fig. 6)

Now put together the down beat, beat to the left, beat to the right, and the up beat to form the four beat measure. (Fig. 7)

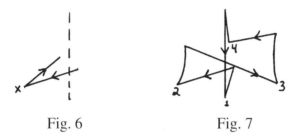

Fig. 6   Fig. 7

There are two types of six beat measures. The fast six is exactly the same as the two beat measure. (See Fig. 3.) The slow six is similar to the four beat measure except that two beats to the left and two beats to the right are used, in addition to the down beat and the up beat. (Fig. 8)

The one beat measure, as it implies, consists of only the down beat. After the ictus is made, proceed directly to the top of the next beat. (Fig. 9)

A distinction should be made, however, in that when the three beat measure is beat in one, as in a fast waltz, the return from making the ictus to the top of the square takes twice as long as going from top to bottom. (Fig. 10)

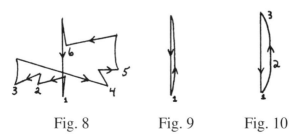

Fig. 8   Fig. 9   Fig. 10

The five beat measure consists of the four beat measure with an added beat to the right or an added beat to the left, according to the pulse of the music. (See Fig. 11.) For a fast tempo combine the two types of one beat measures. (Fig. 12)

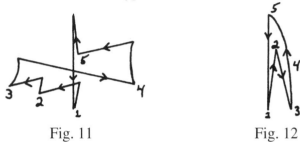

Fig. 11   Fig. 12

When it becomes necessary to subdivide a beat simply add another beat in the same direction as the beat to be subdivided. (Figs. 13, 14, and 15)

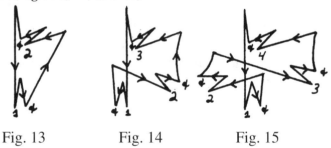

Fig. 13   Fig. 14   Fig. 15

The preparatory beat is used primarily to give the performer an idea of the tempo to follow. It is made at the same speed as the next beat and begins approximately where the ictus of a preceding beat would be. (Figs. 17, 18, 19, and 20)

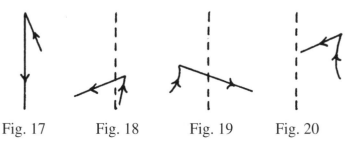

Fig. 17   Fig. 18   Fig. 19   Fig. 20

The hold or pause is made with an inward curving motion. (Fig. 21)

The release or cutoff is made with, an outward curving motion. (Fig. 22)

Fig. 21   Fig. 22

The left hand is used as follows:
a. To reinforce the right hand when making preparatory beats.
b. Changes in tempo.
c. Holds or cuts.
d. Changes in dynamics.
e. Style or character.
f. Cueing performers.

(G) The 26 Essential Drum Rudiments

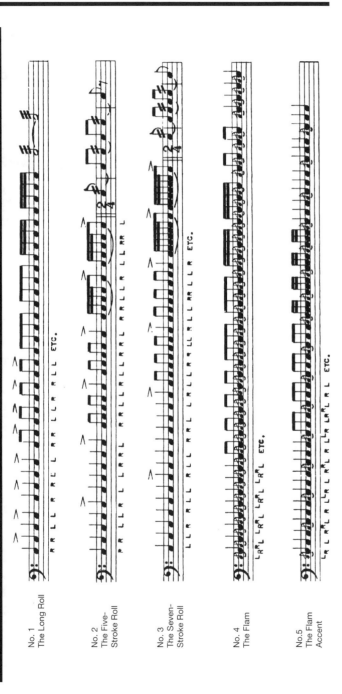

No. 1
The Long Roll

No. 2
The Five-
Stroke Roll

No. 3
The Seven-
Stroke Roll

No. 4
The Flam

No. 5
The Flam
Accent

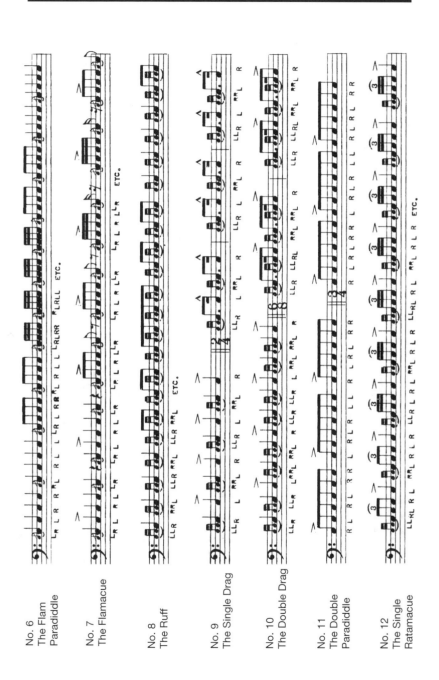

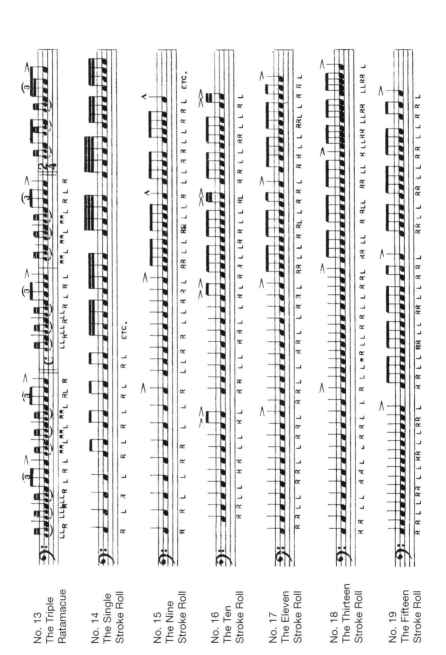

No. 13
The Triple
Ratamacue

No. 14
The Single
Stroke Roll

No. 15
The Nine
Stroke Roll

No. 16
The Ten
Stroke Roll

No. 17
The Eleven
Stroke Roll

No. 18
The Thirteen
Stroke Roll

No. 19
The Fifteen
Stroke Roll

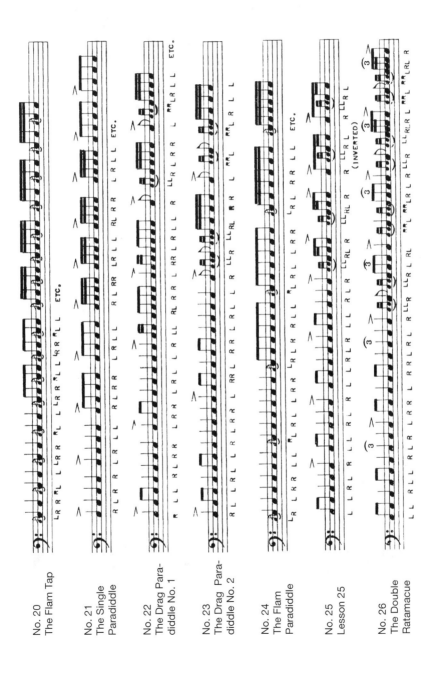

No. 20
The Flam Tap

No. 21
The Single
Paradiddle

No. 22
The Drag Para-
diddle No. 1

No. 23
The Drag Para-
diddle No. 2

No. 24
The Flam
Paradiddle

No. 25
Lesson 25

No. 26
The Double
Ratamacue

(H) The Drum Major

General

The drum major must possess a thorough knowledge of band drill in order to develop a smart marching band. Additionally, he or she must issue commands with spirit, clarity, enthusiasm and decisiveness. The quality of response of the band will directly reflect the manner in which the drum major executes his or her duties.

The drum major issues commands to the band by means of verbal commands and baton signals. In general, verbal commands are used when the band is not in motion or playing, and baton signals are used at all other times. The drum major executes all baton signals while facing front unless otherwise noted.

The baton is the drum major's principal means of communication with the band and consists of a wooden staff approximately four feet long, slightly tapered. A weighted ball is attached to the large end and a tapered ferrule or tip is attached to the other. The wooden shaft may be entwined with cord or chain for decoration. A whistle, if desired, may be used to direct attention to baton signals. The preparatory signal is accompanied by a long blast on the whistle and the execution by a short blast.

Forming the Band

The drum major is responsible for the correct alignment of the marching band. The basic formation of the marching band consists of rows of players called ranks (rows of players extending to the drum major's right and left), and files (rows of players extending from the front to the rear of the band). There should always be more ranks than files, making the band longer or deeper than wide. The space between files is termed "interval," and that between ranks is termed "distance." Both spaces are normally two paces (60 inches). Where limited space is available it may be necessary to narrow the band's front by reducing the "interval" as necessary, but the "distance" should remain two paces.

Position of Drum Major

In basic marching formation, the drum major's position is in front of the center of the leading rank, at a distance in paces equal to the number of men in the band's front rank. When the bandmaster is to conduct the band, the drum major moves to the position normally occupied by the bandmaster. Execution of post changing movements should be accomplished in a precise military manner and with the least possible delay.

Manual of the Baton

Order Baton. The baton is held with the ferrule resting on the ground, on a line with and touching the toe of the right shoe, ball up and to the right. The right arm is extended diagonally to the side, the right hand grasping the staff near the ball with the back of the hand forward. The left hand is on the hip, wrist straight, fingers in front and joined, with the thumb to the rear (Fig. 1).

Parade Rest. The position of "Parade Rest" with the baton is assumed from "Order Baton." The baton remains stationary, while the left foot is moved smartly 12 inches to the left, keeping the legs straight so that the weight of the body rests equally on both feet. At the same time the left hand is placed at the small of the back, palm outward with fingers extended and together (Fig. 2).

Carry Baton. "Carry Baton" is the position of the baton when marching and not marking cadence. The staff is held near the ball with the right hand, the ball alongside the right leg, ferrule up, and the staff resting along the right arm (Fig. 3).

Port Baton. To assume "Port Baton," bring the wrist and arm six inches in front of the chest, holding the baton at a 45° angle across the body with the ferrule up and to the right, the right elbow horizontal with the shoulder (Fig. 4).

Cadence Baton. To establish the proper cadence while the band is marching and performing or to correct tempo discrepancies, the drum major executes "Cadence Baton." The movement, initiated from "Port Baton," is executed in two rhythmic counts as follows: (a) from "Port Baton," the baton is raised diagonally upward and to the right of center (Fig. 5); (b) return the baton to "Port Baton." The position of "Port Baton" will always signify the first, or downbeat, of each musical measure.

Baton Twirl. The twirl may precede all signals. Preparing to execute the twirl, the drum major raises the ball of the baton upward and back so that the staff rests on the arm midway between the shoulders and the elbow, ferrule downward and to the rear, ball upward and to the front. The forearm is held in a vertical position. In executing the twirl, the drum major holds the baton firmly in the fork of the hand formed by the thumb and first finger, with the remaining fingers supporting the staff loosely. By moving the wrist downward and inward, the staff will traverse a circle to the outside of the right arm while the ball traverses a circle between the right hand and the body. Twirls should be made rhythmically in cadence.

Baton Salute. From the position "Order Baton," raise the right arm upward and forward fully extended, to a horizontal position, baton perpendicular, ball up (Fig. 6a). Carry the baton to the left by bending the right elbow so that the back of the hand is touching the left shoulder, arm remaining horizontal (Fig. 6c). Return to "Order Baton" through the reverse of these movements.

From the positions "Carry Baton" or "Cadence Baton," bring the baton to the starting position of the "Twirl," complete the "Twirl" then extend the arm and baton outward and downward to a 45° angle as in figure 6b. Now swing the baton to the left with the back of the hand touching the left shoulder. Return to original position, omitting the twirl.

Baton Signals

Baton signals consist of two basic parts. The preparatory signal indicates the maneuver the band is to perform, while the signal of execution indicates the instant the maneuver is to start.

Forward, March. Preparatory signal: the baton is extended forward and upward at a 45° angle (Fig. 7). Signal of execution: the baton is withdrawn and thrust forcefully in tempo to the position indicated in figure 7.

Mark Time. Preparatory signal: the drum major faces the band, lowers the ferrule to the left, grasps it by the left hand at shoulder level and with both hands thrusts the baton horizontally upward, arms fully extended (Fig. 11a). Signal of execution: the baton is flipped forward by the wrists and returned to the previous position. To resume full step, the drum major faces forward and signals "Forward, March."

Half Step. Preparatory signal: the baton is extended upward in a vertical position and the ferrule lowered to the left until the baton is in a horizontal position overhead. Simultaneously, the left hand, fingers extended and joined, is raised vertically, palm to the right, with the edge of the hand bisecting the baton at approximately the center of the staff. This signal may be given either facing forward or facing the band. Signal of execution: the baton is lowered smartly to shoulder level by bending both elbows. To resume full step, the drum major signals "Forward, March."

Halt. Preparatory signal: same as for "Mark Time," (Fig. 11a). Signal of execution: the baton is lowered to shoulder height on the first beat of a musical measure, thrust horizontally upward on the second beat, and dropped decisively to waist level on the following beat (Fig. 11b). If the band is performing, the drum major immediately executes "Cadence Baton" or "Cease Playing."

Left Turn. Preparatory signal: the baton is extended upward in a vertical position and the ferrule lowered to the left until the baton is in a horizontal position overhead (Fig. 9). Signal of execution: the baton is withdrawn slightly to the right and thrust forcefully to the left in tempo as the left foot strikes the ground.

The drum major completes his left turn, faces the band and comes to "Correct Alignment" until the rear rank of the band has completed its turn. The drum major then faces front and signals "Forward, March."

Right Turn. Preparatory signal: the baton is extended upward in a vertical position and the ferrule lowered to the right until the baton is in a horizontal position above head level (Fig. 10). Signal of execution: the baton is withdrawn slightly to the left and thrust forcefully to the right in tempo as the right foot strikes the ground. The drum major completes his or her right turn, faces the band and comes to "Correct Alignment" as for "Left Turn."

Countermarch. Preparatory signal: the drum major executes "To the Rear" if there are an even number of players in the front rank, or two "Right Turns" if there are an odd number of players in the front rank. He then marks time, and extends the baton upward at a 45° angle in the direction of the countermarch as in "Forward, March." Signal of execution: the baton is withdrawn sharply until ball is against the chest. The signal of execution is given when front rank is two paces distant and as the right foot strikes the ground. The drum major executes "Carry Baton" and steps out at full pace. At the signal of execution, the front rank continues for three steps forward, then executes two "Right Turns" and steps out at full pace between the oncoming files of the band. The following ranks of players execute two "Right Turns" as they reach the pivot point.

Commence Playing. Preparatory signal: the baton is brought to the position of "Port Baton" then extended fully upward at a 45° angle to the right (Fig. 8a). Signal of execution: the baton is dipped in a small arc to the left and upward and returned decisively to "Port Baton" on the downbeat, and continues marking cadence.

Cease Playing. Preparatory signal: same as for "Commence Playing." Signal of execution: the baton is swung to the left in an arc of 90° on the first beat of a musical measure, back to the previous position on the second beat and then lowered decisively to "Port Baton" on the next beat. There is *no* standard baton signal to simultaneously halt the band and cease playing.

Correct Alignment. On occasions requiring the drum major to dress and align the band while marching, he or she will face about, hold the baton with both hands in a horizontal position across the chest and will indicate by short thrusts of the baton to the left or right a correction of interval. By thrusting the baton directly at the band or flipping it toward him- or herself with the wrists, he or she will indicate a shortening or lengthening of the step.

Rendering Honors While Passing in Review. On occasions requiring the band to render honors while passing in review, the drum major will execute "Cease Playing" approximately 10 paces from the Reviewing Officer, execute "Commence Playing" (Ruffles and Flourishes) on the next down-beat and go immediately to "Baton Twirl" and "Baton Salute." The band will complete Ruffles and Flourishes and commence playing the trio of "Anchors Aweigh" or other appropriate music on the next downbeat. The drum major will hold "Baton Salute" until six paces past the Reviewing Officer, then return to "Cadence Baton."

The Sound Off

On the command "Sound Off" by the Adjutant, the drum major verbally commands "Sound Off" and executes "Commence Playing." The band, in place, plays the "Sound Off" and steps off performing a march. After the band has returned to its position, the drum major faces the band and executes "Mark Time" followed by "Halt" and immediately goes to preparatory signal for "Cease Playing." As the band reaches the end of a musical cadence the drum major executes "Cease Playing," followed immediately by the "Sound Off." A musical example of the "Sound Off" is indicated on the following page.

Musical Example of "Sound Off"

The first "Sound Off" is in the key of the first strain of the march which follows.

The second "Sound Off" is in the key of the strain being played as the band returns to its original position.

The following scale degrees are played by the various instruments as indicated:

8-7-8	5-5-5	3-4-3
Flute, Piccolo	3rd B♭ Cornet	2nd Bb Cornet
Oboes, E♭ Clar.	4th Horn in F	1st Horn in F
1st B♭ Clarinet	2nd B♭ Clarinet	1st Alto Saxophone
1st B♭ Cornet		1st Trombone
2nd Horn in F		3rd B♭ Clarinet
B♭ Ten. Saxphone		
2nd Trombone		

1-2-1	1-5-1
3rd Horn in F	E♭ Baritone Saxophone
Euphonium	E♭ Bass Clarinet
2nd Alto Saxophone	3rd Trombone
	BB♭ Basses

Typical Drum Major Positions

Fig. 1
Order Baton

Fig. 2
Parade Rest

Fig. 3
Carry Baton

Fig. 4
Port Baton

Fig. 5
Cadence Baton

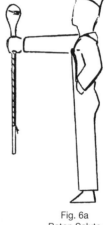

Fig. 6a
Baton Salute
(Count 1 from Order Baton)

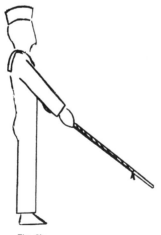

Fig. 6b
Baton Salute
(Count 1 from the Twirl)

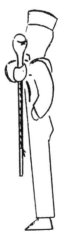

Fig. 6c
Baton Salute

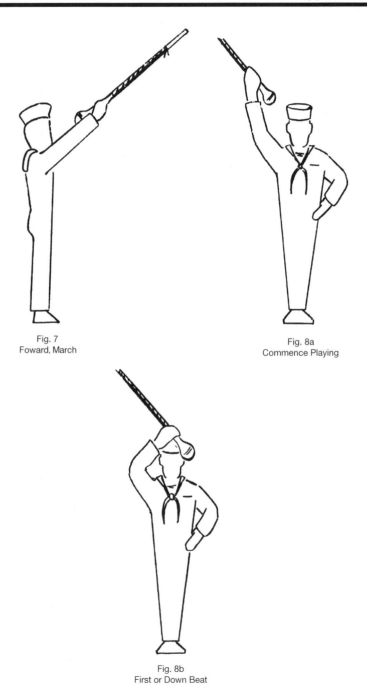

Fig. 7
Foward, March

Fig. 8a
Commence Playing

Fig. 8b
First or Down Beat

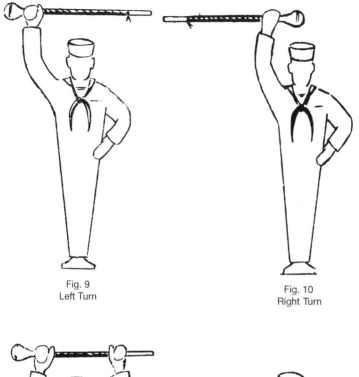

Fig. 9
Left Turn

Fig. 10
Right Turn

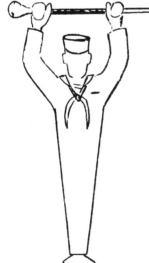

Fig. 11a
Halt (Preparatory);
also Mark Time

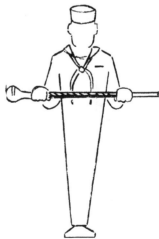

Fig. 11b
Halt (Execution)

(I) Dictionary of Musical Instruments

KEY TO INSTRUMENT PARTS

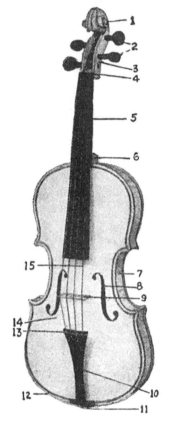

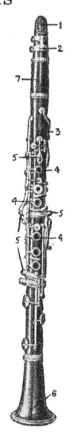

STRING
(Violin)

1. Scroll.
2. Pegs.
3. Peg Box.
4. Nut.
5. Finger Board.
6. Neck Plate.
7. Bout.
8. Sound Hole.
9. Bridge.
10. Tailpiece.
11. Button or Tailpin.
12. Purfling.
13. Lower Nut.
14. Belly.
15. Strings.

WOODWIND
(Clarinet)

1. Mouthpiece (reed is on under side).
2. Ligature or Reedholder.
3. Tube.
4. Rings (Keys).
5. Keys.
6. Bell.
7. Tuning Barrel.

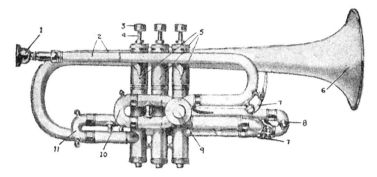

BRASS (Cornet)

1. Mouthpiece.
2. Tube (the entire pipe, from the mouthpiece through all the curves, crooks, and valves to the bell).
3. Valve Button.
4. Piston Rod.
5. Valve Cases (inside of which are the valves).
6. Bell.
7. Water Keys.
8. Tuning and Cleaning Slide.
9. Rotary Valve Change from C to Bb.
10. Tuning and Cleaning Slide.
11. Slide Change from Bb to A.

PERCUSSION (Snare Drum)
(Lower head shown in order to show snares.)

1. Shell.
2. Shell Reinforcement.
3. Flesh Hoop.
4. Counter Hoop.
5. Head (lower).
6. Snares.
7. Snare Strainer.
8. Snare Control (for throwing snare on and off).
9. Tension Rods (for tightening head)

CLASSIFICATION OF MUSICAL INSTRUMENTS

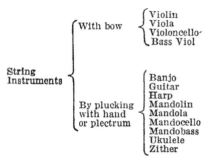

String Instruments

With bow
- Violin
- Viola
- Violoncello
- Bass Viol

By plucking with hand or plectrum
- Banjo
- Guitar
- Harp
- Mandolin
- Mandola
- Mandocello
- Mandobass
- Ukulele
- Zither

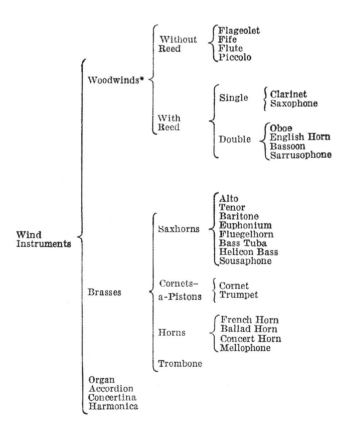

Wind Instruments

Woodwinds*

Without Reed
- Flageolet
- Fife
- Flute
- Piccolo

With Reed

Single
- Clarinet
- Saxophone

Double
- Oboe
- English Horn
- Bassoon
- Sarrusophone

Brasses

Saxhorns
- Alto
- Tenor
- Baritone
- Euphonium
- Fluegelhorn
- Bass Tuba
- Helicon Bass
- Sousaphone

Cornets-a-Pistons
- Cornet
- Trumpet

Horns
- French Horn
- Ballad Horn
- Concert Horn
- Mellophone

Trombone

Organ
Accordion
Concertina
Harmonica

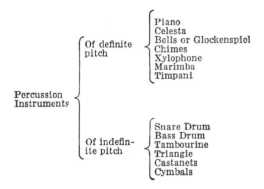

Percussion Instruments

Of definite pitch
- Piano
- Celesta
- Bells or Glockenspiel
- Chimes
- Xylophone
- Marimba
- Timpani

Of indefinite pitch
- Snare Drum
- Bass Drum
- Tambourine
- Triangle
- Castanets
- Cymbals

* *Although called "woodwinds," these are now commonly made of metal with the exception of the oboe, English horn, and bassoon.*

EXPLANATORY NOTES

Because the foreign names of certain instruments are frequently used in instrumental scores, they have been given in the following definitions in Italian (*It.*), German (*G.*), and French (*Fr.*) as well as in English.

The diacritical marks used in the glossary of musical terms indicate the following pronunciations: ā as in ale, â as in care, ă as in am, ä as in arm, ē as in eve, ĕ as in end, ī as in ice, ĭ as in ill, ō as in old, ô as in orb, ŏ as in odd; ū as in use, ŭ as in up, û as in urn.

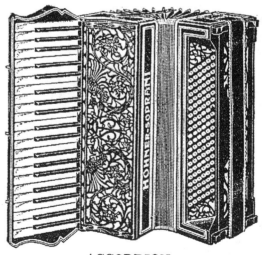

ACCORDION

accordion. (*It.* accordion; *G.* Accordion or Zie-harmonica; *Fr.* accordeon.) A keyed wind instrument in which the wind is forced upon free metallic reeds by means of a bellows. Although it has recently become popular in dance orchestras, it is not a recognized orchestral or band instrument but is used principally for solo or accompaniment purposes. The piano accordion has a piano keyboard of about three and one-half octaves on which the melody is played by the right hand. Under the left hand are a hundred or more bass keys operating several sets of reeds which furnish the accompaniment.

althorn. See ALTO.

alto or **althorn.** The names commonly used for the alto saxhorn in Eb. The alto has a range of about two and one-half octaves and a tone quality which is full, rich, and melodious with considerable power. Its use is principally that of a harmony instrument in bands where it blends perfectly with the woodwinds as well as with the other brasses and yet retains its own power and brilli-

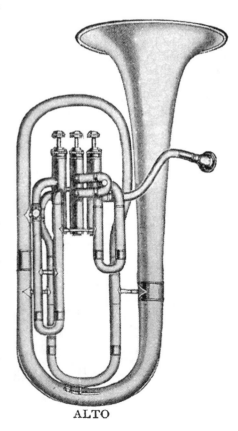

ALTO

ance. The alto is sometimes made in a circular form like a French horn, in which case it is called a mellophone. Music for the alto is written in the G clef. (See SAXHORN and MELLOPHONE.)

alto clarinet. See CLARINET, ALTO.
alto oboe. See ENGLISH HORN.
arigot. See FIFE.
arpa. See HARP.
ballad horn. See MELLOPHONE.
banjo. A fretted stringed instrument having a neck similar to that of a guitar and a body like a drum or tambourine. The regular banjo has five wire strings tuned to D, G, B, D, and G, which are plucked either with the fingers or with a plectrum. The five-stringed banjo is not used in regular orchestras or bands but is used principally as a harmony instrument and for vocal accompaniment. In some instances it is used effectively in solo. A variant, known as the tenor banjo, having only four strings, tuned to C, G, D, and A, is the one used in dance orchestras where it is a a very important instrument. Its snappy, staccato tones accentuate the rhythm admirably.

BANJO (TENOR)

baritone. (Also spelled b a r y - tone.) A deep-toned, t h r e e - valved, b r a s s instrument of the saxhorn family, pitched in Bb an octave lower than the trumpet or cornet and having a range of about three octaves. It is used as a harmony instrument in b o t h orchestra a n d b a n d though occasionally it is used in solo. Music for it is written in the F or b a s s clef. (Also see SAX-HORN and EUPHO-NIUM.)

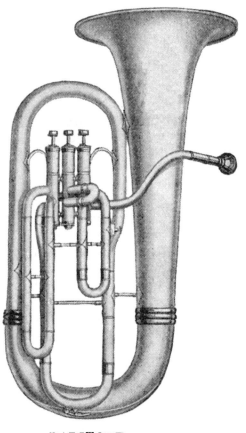

BARITONE

barytone. See BARITONE.

bass. See STRING BASS, also TUBA.

bass clarinet. See CLARINET, BASS.

Bass Klarinette. See CLARINET, BASS.

bass viol. See STRING BASS.

basset horn. (*It.* corno di bassetto; *G.* Basset-horn: *Fr.* cor de basset.) The tenor clarinet in F, until recently considered obsolete but now coming back into use probably because of its excellent tone and ease of execution. It is made and played like the regular clarinet, the principal difference being that it is larger, has a turned up bell of metal like an alto saxophone, and has a leg for resting it on the floor. It is very similar to the alto clarinet in Eb (see illustration of clarinet, alto). The name gives an erroneous impression of the instrument since it is not a horn at all. The inventor, a man named Horn, called his instrument the Basset-Horn meaning "the little bass (clarinet) made by Horn." The basset horn has an unusually large compass— nearly four octaves—and is a transposing instrument written in the treble clef, sounding a fifth lower than written.

bassoon. (*It.* fagotto; *G.* Fagott; *Fr.* bassoon). A deep-voiced wood-wind instrument, the bass of the oboe family. It consists of a tube of conical bore about nine feet long doubled back on itself for facility in handling. Its double-reed mouth-piece is at the end of a metal tube projecting from its side. Its range is about three and one-half octaves, its tone is melancholic. It has three registers, the lower being full and rich, the medium rather colorless and dry, the higher resembling a 'cello. In staccato passages, its dry croaking tones are extremely humorous. The bassoon is a non-transposing instrument pitched in G. Most music for it is written in the bass clef, although the tenor and treble

clefs are sometimes employed. Three bassoons are used in a full symphony orchestra. (Also see BASSOON, DOUBLE.)

bassoon, double. (*It.* contrafagotto; *G.* Kontrafagott: *Fr.* contrebassoon.) The double bassoon or contra bassoon is a huge woodwind instrument almost double the size of the regular bassoon and sounding an octave lower. It is to the oboe family what the double bass is to the violin family. The tube is about sixteen feet long doubled on itself four times to make it easier to handle. Its range is about three octaves, the lower two of which are used principally to extend the downward range of the bassoon. It is pitched in G and music for it is written in the bass clef. Since it sounds an octave lower than written, it is considered a transposing instrument. One only is needed in a grand opera or symphony orchestra.

Becken. See CYMBALS.

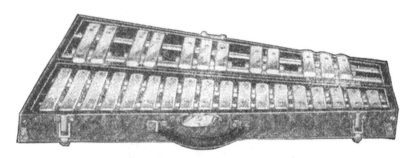

BELLS OR GLOCKENSPIEL

bells. (*It.* campane; *G.* Glockenspeil; *Fr.* cloches.) An orchestral instrument made up of tuned steel bars, rods, or tubes of bell metal mounted on a frame and played by striking with a mallet or mallets. They are graduated in size, the bars and rods giving a tinkling, bell-like sound and the tubes having tones like those of cathedral chimes.

bombardon. See SAXHORN and TUBA.

Bratsche. See VIOLA.

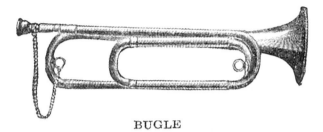

BUGLE

bugle. A brass wind instrument, shorter and more conical than the trumpet. Formerly much used in military bands where it is now superseded by the trumpet and cornet. At the present time it is used principally in military drum and bugle corps and for military call and signal purposes. It has but seven harmonic tones.

bugle tenor. See FLUEGELHORN.

bugles-à-pistons. See SAXHORN.

caisse claire. See DRUM, SNARE.

campane. See BELLS.

cassa. See DRUM, BASS.

castagnettes. See CASTANETS.

castanets. (*It.* castagnette; *G.* Kastagnetten; *Fr.* castagnettes.) A pair of small concave pieces of ivory or hard wood, or sometimes plastic, spoon-shaped and fastened to the thumb by a cord and used by dancers to accent the rhythm. For orchestral purposes, castanets are

CASTANETS

hinged and mounted on a handle. When clapped together they make a dry, clicking sound. They are used by the drummer in the orchestra to accent rhythm and produce characteristic effects, particularly in Spanish dance music.

CELESTA

celesta or **celeste.** A series of graduated steel plates beneath each of which is a tuned wooden resonater. Hammers, operated by a keyboard like that of a piano, strike the plates giving a pleasingly mellow, bell-like tone. The celesta has a range of four octaves. Music for it sounds an octave higher than written. It has recently come into somewhat common use in the orchestra, very effective results being possible when it is played in combination with the wood-winds and strings.

'cello (chĕl'ō) or **violon-cello.** (*It.* violoncello; *G.* Violoncell; *Fr.* violoncelle.) A bass violin having four strings tuned to C, G, D, and A, an octave lower than the viola. Its tone combines the sonority and expressiveness of the violin with a deeper, masculine quality. While its principal purpose is to supply the bass voice of the string choir, its rich tone combined with its great range makes it equally effective in the bass, tenor, or soprano register. In playing, the performer rests the instrument on the floor between his knees. In symphony orchestras there are generally eight or nine, or about half as many 'cellos as first violins. Parts for the 'cello are written in the F or bass clef.

'CELLO

chimes. A set of metal tubes with bell-like tones, tuned to a scale and suspended from a frame. They are used for special chime effects in descriptive music. (See BELLS.)

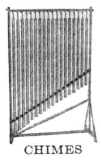

CHIMES

Cinellen. See CYMBALS.

cinelli. See CYMBALS.

clarinet. (*It.* clarinetto; *G.* Klarinette; *Fr.* clarinette.) Specifically, the soprano clarinet, an important woodwind instrument consisting of a cylindrical tube with a bell-shaped opening at one end and a mouthpiece at the other. To the mouthpiece is bound a single reed of cane. The clarinet is in effect a stopped pipe and sounds an octave lower than other woodwinds of the same length. It has holes and keys, by means of which it has a range of three and one-sixth octaves divided into four distinct registers or qualities of tone; rich and sonorous, veiled and feeble, liquid and clear, and shrill. Playing in more than three sharps or flats offers many technical difficulties and, to overcome these, the clarinet is made in several keys, the most common of which are Bb, A, and Eb. It is also made in several sizes,—the large soprano in C, Bb, and A; the small soprano in D, E, F, and Ab; the alto in Eb; the tenor in F, generally called the basset horn; and the bass in C, Bb, and A, an octave lower than the soprano. There are usually two or three clarinets in a symphony orchestra and from ten to thirty in a military band. The clarinet is also an important band instrument, where it supplies the voice taken by the violin in the orchestra. (See also CLARINET, ALTO; CLARINET, BASS; and BASSET HORN.)

CLARI-
NET

clarinet, alto. A clarinet a little larger in size than the soprano, and having a turned up bell like that of an alto saxophone. It is pitched in Eb and sounds a sixth lower than written. It has recently become a very popular band instrument due to its beautiful tone color. By transposing, the alto clarinet may play 'cello, bassoon, French horn, or trombone parts but alto saxophone parts may be used as written.

ALTO
CLARINET

clarinet, bass. (*It.* clarinetto basso; *G.* Bass Klarinette; *Fr.* clarinette basse.) A large clarinet, pitched in Bb an octave lower than the soprano clarinet and shaped similar to a saxophone, with its reed mouthpiece almost at right angles to the tube and its bell turned up. This shape, however, has nothing to do with its tonal quality but is used to make the instrument m o r e convenient to handle. Its tone is deep, full, and organ-like. Only one is needed in a symphony orchestra.

BASS CLARINET

claquebois. See XYLOPHONE.

clarinet, tenor. See BASSET HORN.

clarinette. See CLARINET.

clarinette basse. See CLARINET, BASS.

clarinetto. See CLARINET.

clarinetto basso. See CLARINET, BASS.

cloches. See BELLS.

concert horn. See MELLOPHONE.

concertina. An instrument similar to an accordion but smaller, consisting of an elastic box or bellows, which on being drawn out or compressed, forces air over free reeds on the inside which are controlled by keys on the two hexagonal ends. It has a range of four octaves and and is made in several sizes.

CONCERTINA

contrabass. See TUBA.

contrafagotto. See BASSOON, DOUBLE.

contralto saxhorn. See FLUEGELHORN.

contrebassoon. See BASSOON, DOUBLE.

cor. See HORN.

cor anglais. See ENGLISH HORN.

cor de basset. See BASSET HORN.

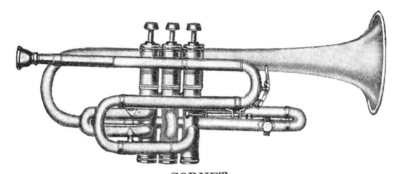

CORNET

cornet. (*It.* cornetto or cornetta; *G.* Kornett; *Fr.* cornet-a-pistons.) Strictly speaking, the **cornet-a-pistons.** A brass wind instrument similar to the trumpet but having a slightly conical instead of a cylindrical tube. It is somewhat shorter and stockier than the trumpet and the inside of the mouthpiece is less cupshaped and more tapering. The tones, which are thicker and more mellow than those of the trumpet, are produced by lipping and the manipulation of three valves. Its range is about two and one-half octaves. In the symphony orchestra and in most of the better orchestras and bands the trumpet is used almost to the exclusion of the cornet, but, due to the comparative ease of playing, it is still popular in small professional and amateur orchestras. The cornet in most common use is pitched in Bb but has a valve mechanism or slide which instantly changes the pitch to A. There is also a cornet pitched in C. Music for the cornet is written in the G or treble clef.

cornet-a-pistons. See CORNET.

cornetta. See CORNET.

cornetto. See CORNET.

corno. See HORN.

corno di bassetto. See BASSET HORN.

corno inglese. See ENGLISH HORN.

cymbales. See CYMBALS.

cymbals. (*It.* piatti or cinelli; *G.* B e c k e n or Cinellen; *Fr.* cymbales.) Pairs of circular metal p l a t e s a b o u t twelve inches in diameter, usually of brass and dish-shaped, with handles at the back. They are used to produce a sharp,

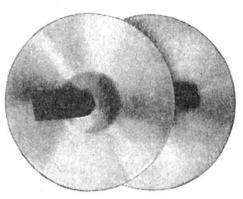

CYMBALS

ringing sound by striking their edges together with a sliding movement. In the dance orchestra, one cymbal is fastened to the bass drum and is struck with each beat of the drum by an arm attached to the pedal mechanism. Another cymbal is suspended over the drum and is struck with a snare drum stick to produce a crash. (See illustration of drums.)

double bass. See STRING BASS, also TUBA.

drum, bass. (*It.* cassa; *G.* Grosse Trommel; *Fr.* grosse caisse.) A percussion instrument consisting of a hollow chamber of wood or metal, usually twenty-six to thirty-two inches in diameter over the ends of which are stretched membranes of skin. When struck with a soft-

headed stick it gives a booming sound without definite pitch. Its principal use is to mark the rhythm. In the larger and symphony orchestras a special bass drummer is employed but in the dance and smaller orchestras the snare drummer also plays the bass drum by means of a pedal. (See illustration.)

drum, snare. (*It.* tamburo militare; *G.* Kleine Trommel; *Fr.* tambour or caisse claire.) Also called the **small** or **side drum.** A percussion instrument consisting of membranes of skin stretched over the ends of a hollow chamber of wood or metal fourteen or fifteen inches in diameter and played with two sticks. It has but one tone, which is determined by the tightness and size of the head. It does not produce a musical tone but is merely of rhythmic value. The snare drum gets its name from thin strings of gut or wire, called snares, which are stretched across its lower head producing its characteristic rattling sound. The snare drum is used in orchestras and bands to accentuate the rhythm and to augment the volume in fortissimo passages.

Englishes Horn. See ENGLISH HORN.

English horn. (*It.* corno inglese; *G.* Englishes Horn; *Fr.* cor anglais.) Not really a horn as its name would seem to indicate but the alto oboe, an instrument quite similar to the oboe in its construction and playing but larger and pitched a fifth lower. It has a knob-shaped instead of a flaring bell. Its tone is deeper,

ENGLISH HORN

richer; and more somber than that of the oboe. It is a transposing instrument, pitched in F, sounding a fifth lower than its notation. Only one English horn is used in the symphony orchestra.

euphonium. A deep‑pitched brass wind instrument of the saxhorn family in Bb, quite similar to the baritone but having a little greater range and a distinct type of tone quality. While the baritone has but three valves, the euphonium has four. Some euphoniums have two tubes played from a single mouthpiece. The smaller one, controlled by the fourth valve, is

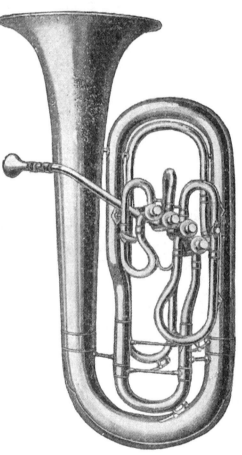

EUPHONIUM

called the trombone or echo bell because of the similarity of its tone quality to that of the trombone. Euphoniums are used in bands almost exclusively, the double-belled instrument being either used as a baritone or by adding the voice of its smaller bell, as a trombone. Music is written in the bass or F clef.

Fagott. See BASSOON.
fagotto. See BASSOON.

FIFE

fife. (*It.* fiffaro; *G.* Pfeife; *Fr.* arigot or fifre.) A six-holed wind instrument of wood or metal with a technique similar to that of a piccolo, but lacking keys and having a range of only two and one-half octaves. It is seldom used in regular orchestras or bands except for military music purposes, but is used chiefly in fife and drum corps.

fiffaro. See FIFE.

fifre. See FIFE.

flauto. See FLUTE.

flauto piccolo. See PICCOLO.

flöte. See FLUTE.

flageolet. A small wind instrument, of either wood or metal, having six holes and a mouthpiece like a whistle. Its tone is shrill but softer than that of a piccolo. Its compass is about two and one-half octaves. (Also see FLUTE)

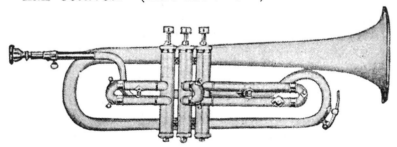

FLUEGELHORN

fluegelhorn. The soprano saxhorn in B or Bb. Sometimes called the **contralto saxhorn** or **bugle tenor.** It is similar in appearance to the trumpet but shorter and stockier, has three valves, and is played like the trumpet. It has a full, rich tone and a range of about two and one-quarter octaves. It is used as a solo as well as a harmony instrument in both orchestras and bands. Music is written in the G clef.

FLUTE

flute. (*It.* flauto; *G.* Flöte; *Fr.* flûte.) A wind instrument consisting of a cylindrical pipe with holes along its length stopped by the fingers or keys. It is closed at the upper end and blown with the mouth across a lateral hole, near the left end. In this respect it differs from all other woodwind instruments, since the others have reeds and are blown through the end of the tube. It is usually made of wood but sometimes of silver or other metal. The usual pitch is in C but there are two others, in Db and G. The flute is made in several sizes, including the piccolo (see PICCOLO) and the flageolet (see FLAGEOLET). Flute music is written in the G clef and sounds as written, since the instrument is non-transposing. Its range is three octaves. The tone is clear and pure. It is especially rich in the lower register and the higher notes are brilliant and piercing. There are usually three flutes in the symphony orchestra.

French horn. See HORN.

Giege. See VIOLIN.

gigelira. See XYLOPHONE.

Glockenspiel. See BELLS.

gong. Also called **tam-tam.** A large round metal plate with the edge turned up, which is struck with a bass drum stick to produce a loud, ringing sound. The drummer in the orchestra uses it in certain fortissimo passages to render a clangorous effect.

grosse caisse. See DRUM, BASS.

Grosse Trommel. See DRUM, BASS.

guitar. A fretted instrument having six wire or gut strings tuned to E, A, D, G, B, and E. It is sometimes used for solo purposes but principally for vocal accompaniment. The tone of the better instruments is harp-like in quality. Sometimes the guitar is equipped with steel strings and a raised bridge and nut, and played by stopping the strings with a steel bar thus producing a weird singing tone. When played in this way, it is called the "steel guitar." There are many variations of the instrument including electric and bass models.

GUITAR

HARMONICA

harmonica. Commonly called the **mouth-organ.** A vibrating metal reed instrument, producing various tones when the breath is inhaled or exhaled through it. It is not an orchestral instrument.

Harfe. See HARP.

harp. (*It.* arpa; *G.* Harfe; *Fr.* harpe.) A stringed instrument consisting of forty-six or forty-seven strings stretched on a triangular frame and tuned to the scale of Cb major. By means of seven pedals which can shift the pitch of the entire set of strings, it is possible to play in any key. The tone is produced by plucking the strings, which are of gut, those of the lower register being wire-spun. The C strings are colored red and the F strings blue to assist the eye.

HARP

Harp music, like that for the piano, is written in both treble and bass clefs. The harp has a range of about six and one-half octaves. Frequently one and sometimes several are used in the symphony orchestra.

harpe. See HARP.
hautbois. See OBOE.
helicon bass. A very large brass wind instrument, pitched in F, Eb, C and Bb, and identical in tone and compass to the tuba but having a circular shape making it convenient to carry over the shoulder. The ease of carrying has brought the helicon into almost universal use in military bands where its size and glittering bell add much to the glamourous appearance. It has also been used much in concert work and has recently been introduced with

HELICON BASS

success in dance orchestras. Music for the helicon bass is written in the bass clef.

hoboe. See OBOE.

FRENCH HORN

horn. (*It.* corno; *G.* Horn; *Fr.* cor.)   A general name for any metal wind instrument consisting of a long tube more or less resembling an ox or ram's horn in shape and in which the lips of the player vibrate against the mouthpiece. Although horn is a general term applied to all of the horn family, specifically it refers to the **French horn,** a brass conical tube about twelve feet long, variously curved, with a flaring bell at one end and a mouthpiece at the other.   It is provided with valves, the use of which in effect lengthen or shorten the tube instantaneously.   The tone is produced by lipping combined with valve manipulation, until a complete chromatic scale is obtainable.   The French horn in F is used almost exclusively.   Its range is about three and one-half octaves and its tone, except when rendered "brassy" by forcing, is pure and mellow and blends perfectly with the woodwinds as well as with the brasses.   It is used both as a harmony and as a melody instrument.   There are usually four French horns in the symphony orchestra. The French horn in F is a transposing instrument; music for it is written in the G or treble clef, the instrument sounding a fifth lower.

kettledrums. See TIMPANI.
Klarinette. See CLARINET.
Kleine Flöte. See PICCOLO.
Kleine Trommel. See DRUM, SNARE.
Kontrafagott. See BASSOON, DOUBLE.
Kornett. See CORNET.

MANDOLIN

mandolin. A fretted instrument having eight strings (four pairs) tuned to E, A, D, and G and played with a plectrum. In the mandolin family there are four instruments, which correspond in size and tuning to the instruments of the violin family. They are the **mandolin** (soprano), the **mandola** (alto or tenor), the **mandocello** (bass), and the **mandobass** (double bass). These instruments are seldom used in regular orchestras but are generally employed in orchestras made up entirely of fretted instruments.

marimba. A xylophone having resonaters hung beneath each of its sound bars. (See XYLOPHONE.)

mellophone, (also spelled **melophone),** **melohorn, concert horn,** or **ballad horn.** A brass wind instrument resembling the French horn in appearance. It is really an alto saxhorn built in a circular form combining the large bore of the alto and its corresponding depth of tone with the flexibility and penetrating mellow tone quality of the French horn. The mellophone is made in several keys, the two most important being the Eb which is principally used in the band and the

EFFECTIVE ORCHESTRAL COMBINATIONS

Number of Players	5	6	7	8	9	10	11	12	13	14	15	16	17	18	19	20	21	22	23	24	25	30	35	40	45	50
Piano (Vocal Edition)	1	1	1	1	1	1	1	1	1																	
1st Violin (9)	1	1	1	1	1	1	1	2	2	2	2	2	2	2	2	3	4	4	4	4	4	4	6	6	8	9
2nd Violin (9 or 10)		1	1	1	1	1	1	1	2	2	2	2	2	2	2	2	2	3	3	3	4	4	4	4	6	7
Viola (11)					1	1	1	1	1	1	1	1	1	1	2	2	2	2	2	2	2	2	4	4	4	6
'Cello (12)	1	1	1	1	1	1	1	1	1	1	1	1	1	1	1	1	1	1	1	2	2	2	2	3	4	4
Bass, String (13)		1	1	1	1	1	1	1	1	1	1	1	1	1	1	1	1	1	1	1	1	2	2	2	2	2
Clarinet (3)	1	1	1	1	1	1	1	1	1	1	2	2	2	2	2	2	2	2	2	2	2	2	2	2	2	2
Piccolo (1)																								1	1	1
Flute (1)							1	1	1	1	1	1	1	1	1	1	1	1	2	2	2	2	2	2	2	2
Oboe (2)													1	1	1	1	1	1	1	1	1	1	1	2	2	2
Bassoon (4)														1	1	1	1	1	1	1	1	1	1	2	2	2
Trumpet (6)	1	1	1	1	1	1	1	1	1	2	2	2	2	2	2	2	2	2	2	2	2	2	3	2	2	2
Trombone (7)			1	1	1	1	1	1	1	1	1	1	1	1	1	1	1	1	1	1	1	3	3	4	3	3
Horn (5)										1	1	2	2	2	2	2	2	2	2	2	2	2	2	4	4	4
Tuba (13)																						1	1	1	1	1
Drums (8)						1	1	1	1	1	1	1	1	1	1	1	1	1	1	1	1	1	1	1	1	1
Timpani (8)																						1	1	1	1	1
Harp (Vocal Edition)																										1

Numbers in parentheses are the numbers of the books of the INSTRUMENTATION OF THE "GOLDEN BOOK" in which the parts are provided.   For complete INSTRUMENTATION list, see page 47.

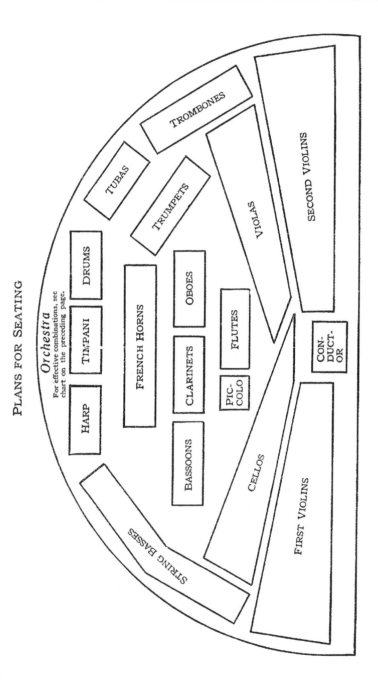

PLANS FOR SEATING

Orchestra

For effective combinations, see chart on the preceding page.

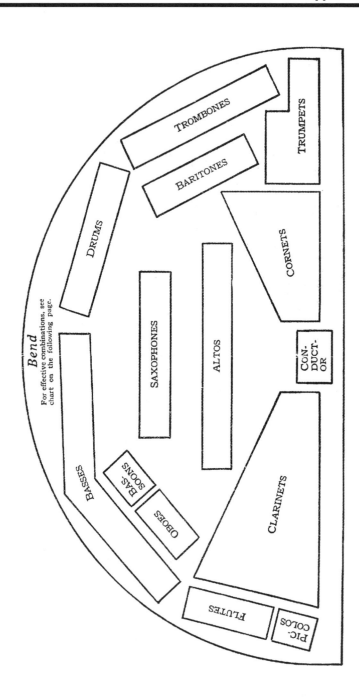

Bend

For effective combinations, see chart on the following page.

EFFECTIVE BAND COMBINATIONS

Number of Players		8	9	10	11	12	13	14	15	16	17	18	19	20	21	22	23	24	25	30	35	40	45	50	60
Cornet or Trumpet	(6)	2	2	2	2	2	2	3	3	3	3	3	3	4	4	4	4	4	4	4	4	4	4	4	4
Horn (Alto)	(16)	2	2	2	2	2	2	2	2	2	2	2	2	2	3	3	3	3	4	4	4	4	4	4	4
Trombone	(17)	2	2	2	2	2	2	2	2	2	2	2	2	2	2	2	2	2	2	3	3	3	3	3	3
Baritone	(12)	1	1	1	1	1	1	1	1	1	1	1	1	1	1	1	1	1	1	1	1	1	2	2	2
Bass (Tuba)	(13)	1	1	1	1	1	1	1	1	1	1	1	2	2	2	2	2	2	2	2	3	4	4	5	6
Clarinet—Bb	(15)		1	2	2	2	3	3	4	4	5	6	6	6	6	7	7	7	7	9	11	14	17	19	24
Clarinet—Eb	(14)																					1	1	2	2
Soprano Saxophone	(6)																								1
Alto Saxophone	(4)																1	1	1	1	1	1	1	1	1
Tenor Saxophone	(4)																	1	1	1	1	1	1	1	1
Baritone Saxophone	(4)																			1	1	1	1	1	1
Bass Saxophone	(4)																							1	1
Piccolo—Db	(14)									1	1	1	1	1	1	1	1	1	1	1	1	1	1	1	2
Flute	(1)																			1	1	1	1	1	1
Oboe	(2)																				1	1	1	1	2
Bassoon	(4)																					1	1	1	2
Drums	(8)			1	1	2	2	2	2	2	2	2	2	2	2	2	2	2	2	2	2	2	3	3	3

Numbers in parentheses are the numbers of the books of the INSTRUMENTATION OF THE "GOLDEN BOOK" in which the parts are provided. For complete INSTRUMENTATION list, see page 47.

MELLOPHONE

F which is the most popular orchestral mellophone. The range is about two and one-half
octaves. Music for the mellophone is written
in the treble clef and within the same range as
the alto or French horn; in fact, the Eb instrument may substitute for the alto in the band and
the F instrument may substitute for the French
horn in the orchestra.

mouth organ. See HARMONICA.

1. VIOLIN MUTE OR SORDINO

2. TRUMPET OR CORNET MUTE

mute. (1) A device that can be clasped on the bridge of a violin, or similar instrument, to deaden or soften the tone. This is sometimes called a **sordino.** (2) A pear-shaped pad that can be inserted in the bell of a metal wind instrument to muffle the tone. Some brass players also use a "plunger" style rubber mute to muffle their instruments.

oboe. (*It.* oboe; *G.* Hoboe; *Fr.* hautbois.) A woodwind instrument about the size of a clarinet, consisting of a tube, with a conical bore, a slightly flaring bell, and finger holes and keys. The mouthpiece is a double reed made of two very thin pieces of cane bound together in such a way as to leave a small opening between them, through which the air is blown, setting them into vibration and producing the sound. The fingering is somewhat like that of the flute. It is a non-transposing instrument, pitched in C and having a range of about two and one-half octaves, all in the soprano register. The tone is reedy, nasal, and quaint, and adaptable to pastoral and melancholy effects. In the symphony orchestra, two and sometimes three oboes are used. In the oboe family, distinguished by its double-reed mouthpiece, there are four instruments, the oboe or soprano, the English horn or alto, the bassoon or bass, and the double bassoon or contrabass.

OBOE

ocarina. A small simple wind instrument having an oval terra cotta body, a mouthpiece and finger holes, and producing a fluty tone. It is made in four sizes, making it possible to play in quartettes.

OCARINA

AN ORGAN CONSOLE

organ. Specifically the **pipe organ.** A wind instrument which in its most modern and complete form is the largest, most powerful, and most varied in its resources of all musical instruments. It is capable of almost all the powers and qualities of nearly all other instruments. To attempt to describe the organ in detail would be entirely beyond the scope of this booklet but briefly it consists of many sets of pipes of metal, reed, or wood sounded by compressed air from bellows and controlled by keyboards and drawknobs. The pipes are grouped into registers or stops, each group being of uniform quality of tone and furnishing a complete scale. The pipes are like huge flutes, oboes, or trumpets, etc., each having its own mechanism to operate it and its one particular tone to produce. There are from one to five keyboards or manuals for the hands and a pedal keyboard operated by the feet which control separate sets of pipes known as the Great Organ, Swell Organ, Choir, Solo, Pedal, and Echo Organ. The visible part of the organ consisting of the manuals, stops, pedals, wooden case, etc., is known as the console (see illustration). By means of combining many stops and using one or more manuals at the same time, what would be a simple tone or chord on any other instrument may become a vast group of tones of various pitches and colors.

ottavino. See PICCOLO.

petite flûte. See PICCOLO.

pfeife. See FIFE.

piano. From the Italian word, pianoforte. Commonly abbreviated to **piano.** A stringed percussion instrument giving its tones from steel wires which are struck by hammers operated by a keyboard. The essential parts of the piano are: the **frame,** usually of cast iron in one piece and made to resist the tension of the strings, which amounts to twelve to twenty tons; the **soundboard,** by which the sonorousness is increased and the tone quality improved;

PIANO

the **action,** which comprises the mechanism con-
necting the keyboard and hammers; the **strings** or
wires graduated in length and thickness so as to
produce the desired variations in tone; the **keyboard,** consisting of white keys forming the scale
of C and black keys furnishing all necessary
semitones to command the major and minor scales;
the **dampers,** which regulate the volume of tone
and are operated by the pedals; and the **case.** The
piano has a complete chromatic scale with a range
of about seven and one half octaves. Music for the
piano is written on both the treble and bass clefs.
No other instrument except the organ approaches
its resources in chords, range, and brilliance. The
piano is used in nearly all theater, dance, amateur,
and small orchestras but seldom in the symphony
orchestra. It is equally adaptable for solo or accompaniment purposes, but should be considered primarily as a solo instrument.

piatti. See CYMBALS.

PICCOLO

piccolo. (*It.* flauto piccolo or ottavino; *G.* Kleine Flöte; *Fr.* petite flûte.) A half-sized flute pitched an octave higher than the regular flute and played similarly. Its tone is clear and piercing and lends brilliancy to many passages. In the orchestra, its principal use is to extend the range of the flutes. It is made in C and Db.

pipe organ. See ORGAN.

Posaune. See TROMBONE, SLIDE.

sarrusophone. A brass wind instrument resembling a bassoon in appearance but made of metal. It is made in several sizes and is used principally in military bands. The tone is like that of the trombone and blends with either the other brasses or the woodwinds, adding considerably to the tonal volume of the ensemble.

sassaphone. See SAXOPHONE.

SARRUSOPHONE

saxhorn. Any of a family of brass wind instruments having a long, winding tube of conical bore with a wide bell opening, and three to five valves. Invented about 1845 by Adolphe Sax. Saxhorns are made in many sizes, and are divided into two groups, the **bugles-a-pistons** and the **tubas** or **bombardons.** Of the first group the most common are: the soprano saxhorn in B or Bb, usually called the fluegelhorn (see FLUEGELHORN), the alto saxhorn or mellophone in Eb (see ALTO, also MELLOPHONE), and the tenor saxhorn in Bb (see TENOR). Of the tuba, or bombardon group, the most common are: the bass saxhorn in Bb, usually called the euphonium or baritone (see EUPHONIUM, also BARITONE); the low bass saxhorn in Bb, Eb, or F, commonly called the tuba (see TUBA); and the contrabass saxhorn in Bb or Eb, usually called the double Bb or double Eb bass.

saxophone. (*It.* sassophone; *G.* Saxophone; *Fr.* saxophone.) A keyed wind instrument named for its inventor, Adolphe Sax, combining the single reed mouthpiece of the clarinet with a conical tube of metal. The tone is similar to that of the 'cello and yet to that of the clarinet. It is a transposing instrument for which music is written in the G or treble clef. Saxophones are made in several sizes, the range of each being nearly three octaves. The most common sizes and keys are: the soprano in Bb, alto in Eb, tenor in Bb or in C (usually called C melody), baritone in Eb, and bass in Bb. The saxophone has become the outstanding instrument in modern popular music and is used principally in dance, amateur, and

STRAIGHT
SOPRANO
SAXOPHONE

small orchestras, and in military bands, but seldom in the symphony orchestra. The most popular of the several sizes and keys is the alto in Eb.

Schellen Trommel. See
TAMBOURINE.
side drum. See DRUM, SNARE.
slide trombone. See TROMBONE, SLIDE.
small drum. See DRUM, SNARE.
sordino. See MUTE.

sousaphone. A huge bass brass wind instrument in Eb or Bb having three valves, similar in appearance to the helicon bass with its circular shape but having a larger and more flaring bell. Its tones are deep and organ-like. It is principally a military band instrument, but is often used in dance orchestras.

ALTO SAXOPHONE

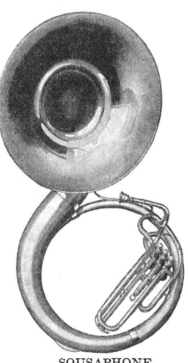

SOUSAPHONE

string bass. Also called **double bass, bass,** or **bass viol.** (*It.* contrabasso or violone; *G.* Kontrabass; *Fr.* contre-basse or violonar.) The largest and deepest toned of the viol family. Its four strings are tuned to E, A, D, and G—not in fifths as are other instruments of the viol class, but in fourths to facilitate handling. Music for the bass is written on the F or bass clef but the actual sound is an octave lower. To this instrument falls the playing of the lowest tones of the score. While being played, the instrument stands on the floor, the player standing at the side and behind it. It is taller than the average

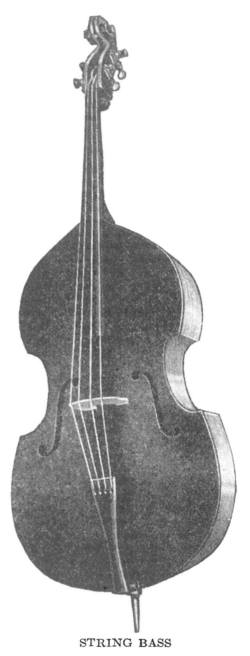

STRING BASS

man. In symphony orchestras there are usually two less string basses than 'cellos.

Strohfiedel. See XYLOPHONE.

tambour. See DRUM, SNARE.

tambour de basque. See TAMBOURINE.

Tambourin. See TAMBOURINE.

tambourine. (*It.* tambu-rino; *G.* Tambourin or Schellen Trommel; *Fr.* tambour de basque). A small drum-like percussion instrument with but one head and metal discs,

TAMBOURINE

called jingles, inserted in openings in the frame. When the head of the tambourine is struck with the hand, the instrument gives a sound like a drum accompanied by the rattle of the jingles, or by shaking the instrument without striking the head, the jingles may be trilled. The drummer in the orchestra uses the tambourine to produce characteristic effects in oriental or barbaric music and sometimes in Spanish dance music.

tamburino. See TAMBOURINE.

tamburo militare. See DRUM, SNARE.

tam-tam. See GONG.

tenor. The tenor saxhorn in Bb (see SAXHORN). It is larger than an alto and smaller than a baritone and has a range of about two and one-half octaves. It is used only in bands, principally as a harmony instrument to add tenor voice coloring. Music for the tenor is written in the G clef.

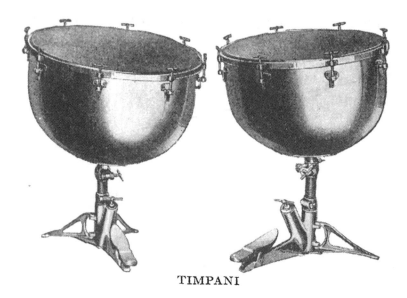

TIMPANI

timpani. (*It.* timpani; *G.* Pauken; *Fr.* timbales.) (Sometimes spelled **tympani** or **tympany.**) Also called **kettledrums.** Hemispherical bowls of brass or copper, over the tops of which are stretched heads of vellum, tightened by rings and tuned by screws or by cords and braces. They are usually played in pairs with two sticks having flexible handles and soft knobs. The pair consists of a large and a small drum, the large one having a range from F to C and the small one from Bb to F. The latest timpani are equipped with pedal mechanisms to vary the pitch but this is generally done by means of the tuning screws. Timpani are used for accentuating the rhythm and to add life and motion to sustained chords. One set is always used in the symphony orchestra and sometimes two sets.

Triangel. See TRIANGLE.

triangle. (*It.* triangolo; *G.* Triangel; *Fr.* triangle.) A percussion instrument, made of steel and bent into the form of a triangle open at one angle and hung by a cord. When struck with a metallic rod, it gives a clear and tinkling sound. The triangle is used by the drummer to mark the rhythm and sometimes to produce a trill by striking two sides of the instrument alternately. (For illustration, see DRUMS.)

triangolo. See TRIANGLE.
trombo clarino. See TRUMPET.

SLIDE TROMBONE

trombone, slide. (*It.* trombone; *G.* Posaune; *Fr.* trombone.) A powerful brass instrument of the trumpet family consisting of a tube in three parts bent twice upon itself and ending in a bell. The U-shaped middle section slides into the two end sections in a telescopic fashion adjusting the length of the tube and its consequent pitch. It can slide from note to note as smoothly as a violin. Its tone is of the utmost dignity and richness. The trombone possesses every shading of volume from a most exquisite pianissimo to a fortissimo surpassing that of any other brass instrument. The trombone is the tenor voice of the metal quartette. It is made in four sizes, the tenor in Bb being used almost exclusively. The range is about three octaves. Three trombones are used in the symphony orchestra, all three usually being tenor instruments, but sometimes one of them is a bass in G. For the notation the bass clef is generally used although parts are sometimes written in the tenor clef. The trombone is usually treated as a non-transposing instrument. (Also see TROMBONE, VALVE.)

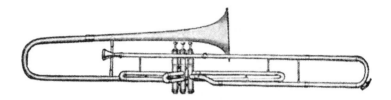

VALVE TROMBONE

trombone, valve. A brass wind instrument having the same length tube as the slide trombone
and a similar tone quality but three valves instead
of a slide to produce the scale. It is not in very
common use, except among beginners and student
organizations, the only advantage over the slide
trombone being ease of execution. Music for
the valve trombone is the same as that for the
slide trombone. (See TROMBONE, SLIDE.)

Trompete. See TRUMPET.

trompette. See TRUMPET.

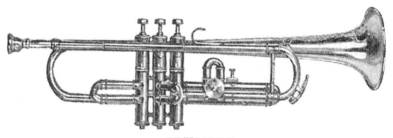

TRUMPET

trumpet. (*It.* tromba clarino; *G.* Trompete;
Fr. trompette.) A brass wind instrument having
a cylindrical tube one-half as long as that of the
French horn and therefore pitched an octave

higher. The inside of the mouthpiece is hemi-spherical and cupped, the tone being produced by lipping and the manipulation of three valves. Its compass is about three octaves, its tone quality brilliant and penetrating. The trumpet is pitched in Bb but, by a slide or valve mechanism, it may be instantly lowered to A. There are also trumpets pitched in other keys but they are obsolete and seldom used. The trumpet is the leading voice of the brass choir. In the symphony orchestra two, three, and sometimes four trumpets are used.

tuba, bass, double bass, contrabass, bombardon. The lowest pitched of the saxhorns, enormous brass wind instruments with three to five valves, a trombone-like mouthpiece, and ranges of about four octaves. There are three tuba sizes: the bass saxhorn (usually called the baritone or euphonium) in Bb; the low bass saxhorn or bombardon in Bb, Eb, or F; and the

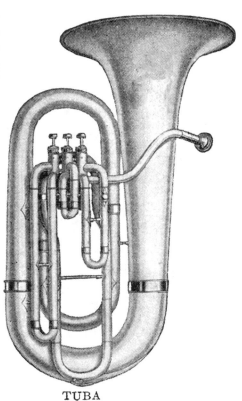

TUBA

contrabass saxhorn in Bb, Eb, or C. Their soft organ-like tones blend exceedingly well, the smaller sizes being used for orchestral purposes and the larger sizes for band. The tuba is the double bass of the brass section of the orchestra, one, or two at most, being necessary in the symphony orchestra. Although the tuba is made in several keys, it is invariably treated as a non-transposing instrument.

tympani. See TIMPANI.

ukelele. A fretted four-stringed Hawaiian musical instrument usually tuned to A, D, F#, and B. It is similar in shape to a guitar but much smaller in size. Used principally for vocal accompaniment. Not an orchestral instrument but sometimes used in groups made up exclusively of fretted instruments. It is also made in the form of a banjo, called a **banjo ukulele,** having a banjo body with a ukelele keyboard.

viol. See VIOLA, VIOLIN, VIOLONCELLO, and STRING BASS.

UKELELE

viola. (*It.* viola; *G.* Bratsche; *Fr.* viole). The tenor voice of the string choir. Similar in appearance to the violin, but somewhat larger. It is tuned a fifth lower than the violin, its four strings being tuned to C, G, D, and A. Its strings are rather thick, the lower two being wire-wound. The tone of the viola is somber, with an elegiac quality. In the orchestra the viola is most frequently employed as a harmony instrument and in the symphony orchestra there are generally ten or about three-quarters as many violas as second violins. Music for the viola is written in the C or tenor clef.

viole. See VIOLA.

violin. (*It.* violino; *G.* Violine or Geige; *Fr.* violon.) The most important of the stringed instruments of the viol class, having four strings tuned to G, D, A, and E. Its range is over four octaves. Due to the brilliancy, power, and expressiveness of its tones, it has become the leading instrument of the orchestra as well as one of the most popular solo instruments of the concert stage. It is made of carefully selected woods; and in the better instruments, every detail of adjustment between bridge, sound posts, and sound holes, and of model, joining, and varnish, is studied to bring about the utmost sonority and refinement of tone. The lower three strings are made of gut, the lowest or G string being overspun with silver or gold wire. The E string is now usually of steel both

VIOLIN

because of the purity of its tone color and wearing quality. However, some violinists still use one of gut. The bow is strung with fine horsehair and rubbed with rosin to make it "bite." The fingers act as hammers on the strings to stop out the desired tones which are produced by drawing the bow across one or more of the strings. There are usually about thirty violins in a full symphony orchestra, about sixteen playing first violin and fourteen playing second. Music for the violin is written in the G or treble clef.

Violine. See VIOLIN.

violino. See VIOLIN.

violon. See VIOLIN.

violoncello. See 'CELLO.

xilophone. See XYLOPHONE.

xylaphon. See XYLOPHONE.

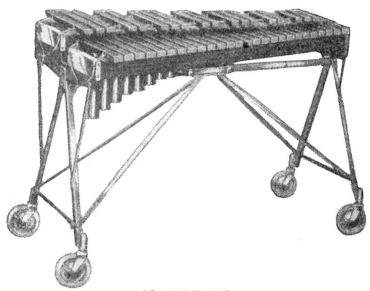

XYLOPHONE

xylophone (zī′lŏ-fŏn) (*It.* xilophone or gigelira; *G.* Xylophone or Strohfiedel; *Fr.* xylaphon or claquebois.) An instrument consisting of a series of graduated bars of wood mounted on stretched cords in a frame. There are thirty or more bars, chromatically tuned and arranged in two rows. When struck with mallets, the bars produce a hard, hollow tone. The xylophone is used frequently in dance and theater orchestras and occasionally in the symphony orchestra. When resonators are hung beneath the tone-producing bars, the xylophone is called a **marimba.**

Zieharmonica. See ACCORDION.

zither. An instrument having about thirty-six strings of wire or gut stretched over a shallow sound-box. At one side under five of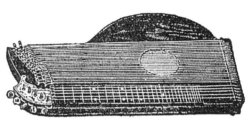

ZITHER

the strings is a fretted finger board like that of a guitar, on which the melody is stopped out by the left hand and played by a plectrum attached to the right thumb. The other strings are tuned in fourths and are plucked by the fingers of the right hand to furnish an accompaniment.

GLOSSARY OF MUSICAL TERMS

Including only those terms of frequent occurence in music intended for school use. Pronunciation is not indicated for terms pronounced phonetically.

a capella or **alla capella** (äl-lä käp-pāl'lä). Vocal chorus without accompaniment.

accelerando or **accel.** (ät-tschĕl-ā-rän'dō). Quickening speed gradually.

accent. The regularly recurring stress upon a tone to mark the beginning, and more feebly, the third part of a measure.

accidental. A sharp, double sharp, flat, double flat, or natural not a part of the signature.

accompaniment. The part of a musical composition which supports the melody or theme.
adagio (ä-dä′djō). Slowly. Leisurely.
adagio assai (ä-dä′djō äs-sä-ē). Very slow.
adagio non troppo (ä-dä′djō nŏn trŏp′pō). Not too slow.
ad libitum or **ad lib.** (äd lĭb′-ĭ-tŭm). At liberty. At pleasure.
agitato (ä-djē-tä′tō). Perturbed. Agitated.
al fine (äl fē′nĕ). To the end.
allegretto (äl-lĕ-grāt′tō). Lively.
allegro (äl-lā′grō). Quick.
allegro moderato (äl-lā′grō mŏd-ä-rä′tō). Moderately fast.
all'ottava (äl lŏt-tä′vä). An octave above or below.
alto. The deeper of the two principal divisions of women's or boys' voices. See also ALTO in musical instrument section.
andante (än-dän′tĕ). Slow, but not so slow as adagio. An easy graceful movement.
andantino (än-dän-tē′-nō). Slightly quicker than andante.
animato (ä-nē-mä′-tō). With animation.
arco. The bow. Resume the bow (after pizzacato).
arpeggio (är-pä-djō). In harp style. The notes of the chord not to be struck simultaneously, but in quick succession upward.
a tempo or **tem.** (ä tām′pō). Resume time.
barcarolle. A composition similar in character to the songs of the Venetian gondoliers.
baritone (or **barytone**). The voice higher than bass and lower than tenor. See also BARITONE in musical instrument section.
bass (bāss). The lowest male adult voice. The lowest part of a musical composition. See also **bass** in musical instrument section.
bolero. A lively Spanish dance.
brillante (brēll-yän′tĕ). Brilliantly.

cadence. A closing or ending of a piece or phrase.

cantabile (kän-tä′bē-lä). In a singing style.

canto. A song.

capriccio (kä-prē′tchō). Quick. Capricious.

chord. Two or more notes combined according to harmonic principles.

clef. A symbol to indicate the placement of the notes on the staff. The most common clefs are the treble or G clef which places G on the second line; the tenor or alto clef the center point of which marks middle C, sometimes on the first or fourth line but most often on the third line as in viola music; and the bass or F clef which places F on the fourth line.

coda (kō′dä). A passage appended as a definite conclusion to a piece of which some portions have been repeated.

coloratura (kŏ-lŏ-rä-too′rä). Trills or runs added to a vocal or instrumental composition to give brilliancy.

con brio (kŏn brē′ō). With vigor, force.

con fuoco (kŏn fwō′kō). With fire. With spirit.

con moto (kŏn mō′tō). With spirited motion.

contralto. The highest male or lowest female voice. The voice or singer performing the part.

crescendo or **cresc.** (krā-shän′dō). Gradually increasing the power of the tone.

da capo or **D. C.** (dä kä′pō). (Repeat) "from the beginning."

dal segno or **D. S.** (däl sän-yō). (Repeat) "from the sign." It indicates that a part of the composition is to be repeated beginning at the sign and ending with *Fine*.

decrescendo or **decresc.** (dä-krā-shän′dō). Gradually decreasing the power of the tone.

diminuendo or **dimin.** (dē-mē-noo än′ dō). Same as decrescendo.

divisi or **div.** Separately.

dolce (dōl′chĕ). Soft and sweet.

dot. At the right of a note, increases its value by one-half. Above or below a note, indicates staccato.

f. See FORTE.

ff. See FORTISSIMO.

fff. See FORTISSISIMO.

falsetto (fäl-sĕt'tō). A false or artifical voice. That voice in a man which lies above his natural voice.

fermata or **fermate** (fär-mä'tä). A hold. A pause.

figure. Any short succession of notes which produces a single, complete, and distinct impression.

finale (fē-nä'lĕ). The last movement of a composition.

fine (fē'nē). The end.

flat. Below pitch. A character signifying that notes before which it appears are to be played or sung a half-step lower than written on the staff.

flat, double. A character signifying that the note before which it appears is to be played or sung two half-steps lower than written on the staff.

forte or **f.** (fōr'tĕ). Loud.

forte-piano or **fp.** Loud, then soft.

fortissimo or **ff.** (fōr-tēs'sē-mō). Very loud.

fortissisimo or **fff.** As loud as possible.

forzando or **forz.** or **fz.** (fōr-tsän'dō). Strong accent on the note or chord over which the sign appears.

fp. See FORTE-PIANO.

fz. See FORZANDO.

glissando (glē-sän-dō). A gliding effect produced by sliding the finger along or over the strings or keys.

grace. A note with little or no time value.

grandioso (grän-dyō'zō). Grand. Noble.

grave (grä'vĕ). Serious and slow.

harmony. The concord of two or more sounds or strains which differ in pitch and quality.

hold. A sign, the fermata, placed over or under a note or rest indicating that it is to be prolonged.

intermezzo (ĭn-târ-mād′sō). A short intermediate movement in a symphony.

larghetto (lär-gät′tō). Not quite so slow as largo.

larghissimo (lär-gēs′sē-mō). Slower than largo.

largo (lärgō). Slow.

legatissimo (lĕ-gä-tēs′sē-mō). Very smooth and connected.

legato (lā-gä′tō). Smooth and connected. Tied.

lentissimo (lān-tē′sē-mō). Very slow.

lento (lān′tō). Slow.

m. See MEZZO.

mf. See MEZZO-FORTE.

maestoso (mä-ĕs-tō′sō). Majestic. Dignified.

marcia. In march style.

mezza or **mezzo** (mā′dsō). Half.

mezza voce (mädsä vō′chĕ). Half power. Half voice.

mezzo forte or **mf.** (mā′dsō fōr′tĕ). Half as loud as forte.

mezzo piano or **mp.** (mā′dsō pē-ä′nō). Not so soft as piano.

mezzo soprano (mā′dsō sō-prä′nō). The female voice between the alto and the soprano.

moderato (mŏd-ā-rä′tō). Moderate.

mp. See MEZZO-PIANO.

mute. See musical instrument section.

natural. A character cancelling within a measure a preceding sharp or flat.

obbligato (ŏb-blĭ-gä′tō). Required. Necessary. Indispensible. A part indispensible to the just performance of a composition.

octave. An interval of seven degrees between any note and the corresponding note above or below it. The tone next above or below that has the same letter-name.

opus or **op.** (ō′pŭs). A work.

p. See PIANO.

pp. See PIANISSIMO.

ppp. See PIANISSISIMO.

pianissimo or **pp.** (pē-än'ĭs-sē-mō). Very soft.

pianissisimo or **ppp.** Barely audible.

piano or **p.** (pē-ä'nō). Soft.

pitch. The highness or lowness of a tone (not the softness or loudness).

pizzicato or **piz.** (pēt-sē-kä'tō). Very staccato. In music for stringed instruments, it means that the portion of the music so marked is to be played by plucking, and not by bowing.

poco a poco (pō'kō ä pō'kō). Little by little.

prestissimo (präs-tē'sē-mō). As fast as possible.

presto (präs'tō). Faster than allegro, but slower than prestissimo.

prima donna (prē'mä dŏn'nä). The leading soprano in an opera.

rallentando or **rall.** (räl-län-tän'dō). Gradually decreasing the speed.

repeat. Repeat the chord or figure.

rf. or **rfz.** See RINFORZANDO

rinforzando, or **rin.,** or **rinf.,** or **rf.,** or **rfz.** (rēn-fōr-tsän'dō). Same as forzando.

ritardando or **ritard.** (rē-tär-dän'dō). Same as rallentando.

ritenuto, or **rit.,** or **riten.** (rē-tā-noo'tō). Slightly slower time.

scherzando (skâr-tsän'dō). In a lively, playful style.

scherzo (skâr'tsō). A composition or movement of playful, lively character.

sforzato or **sf.** (sfôr-tsä'tō). Same as forzándo.

sharp. A character signifying that notes before which it appears are to be played or sung a half-step higher than written on the staff.

sharp, double. A character signifying that the notes before which it appears are to be played or sung two half-steps higher than written on the staff.

simile. Similarly. An indication that a certain manner of playing is to continue until otherwise indicated.

slur. The symbol placed over or under two or more notes to indicate that the passage is to be played legato.

solo (sō′lō). Rendition by a single instrument or voice with or without accompaniment.

smorzando (smŏr-tsän′dō). Gradually dying away.

soprano (sō-prä-nō). The higher of the two principal divisions of women's or boys' voices.

sordino (sōr-dē′nō). Mute. See MUTE in musical instrument section.

sostenuto (sŏs-tä-noo′tō). Sustained.

spirito (spē′rē-tō). Spirited. Lively.

staccato (stäk-kä′tō). A note produced by a touch which leaves the key or string instantly. Staccato playing is indicated by a dot or a dash placed over the notes, the dash indicating shorter duration than the dot.

swell. A name for the crescendo symbol.

tacet. Be silent.

tem. See A TEMPO.

tenor. The highest male adult voice.

tie. A curved line joining two notes of the same pitch: to be distinguished from the slur, which joins two or more notes of various pitches.

time. The grouping into equal measures of successive rhythmic beats or pulsations according to accentuation. For the different note-values and accentuations there are different kinds of time, indicated by such figures as $\frac{4}{4}$. The denominator indicates the kind of counts (note value), and the numerator the number of counts to the measure. In other words, $\frac{4}{4}$ means that there are four quarter notes, or their equivalent, to the measure.

tone. A musical sound.

tremolo (trā′mō-lō). A quivering effect. Trembling. Repeated with great rapidity.

triad. A common chord, consisting of a root, third, and fifth.

sul. On. As "sul G," on the G string.

trill or **tr.** A musical embellishment.

triplet. A group of three notes sung or played in the time of one.

tutti (toot′tē). All. The entire number of players or singers.

unison or **unis.** The same pitch of sounds played by two or more instruments or sung by two or more voices.

veloce (vē-lō′chĕ). Quick. Rapid.

vivace (vē-vä′chĕ). Quick. Lively.

turn. An embellishment consisting of four tones, a principal tone struck twice and the tone above and below it struck once.

SIGNS AND SYMBOLS

(For unfamiliar terms, see glossary, page 40.)

. Dot. Staccato.

⌢⋅⋅ Slightly staccato.

▲▼ Very staccato.

⌒ Fermate. Hold.

𝄋 Segno. Sign used to mark the point to which reference is made or at which the repetition of a passage is to begin.

♯   Sharp.

𝄪   Double sharp.

♭   Flat.

♮   Natural.

◁ Crescendo.

▷ Diminuendo.

⌒ Legato. Slur. Tie.

V   Up bow. Breathing place.

Λ   Accent.

⊓   Down bow.

∿   Continue the trill.

{   Arpeggio.

≣ Single bar. Used to indicate regular measure

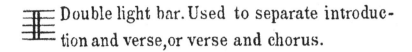 Double light bar. Used to separate introduction and verse, or verse and chorus.

Light and heavy bar. Used at *Fine*.

 Brace. Used to indicate duration of a passage.

G or treble clef.   See *clef*.

F or bass clef   See *clef*.

C or alto clef. See *clef*.

 Pesante or Tenuto.

3   Rest of one or more measures, the figure indicating the number of measures.

8va   Ottavo alta. The octave above.

8va bassa   Ottavo bassa. The octave below.

fp   Forte-piano.

‖: :‖   Repeat the inclosed section.

⅟.   Repeat the preceding measure.

⌢3   Triplet.

C   Common time. Same as $\frac{4}{4}$ but sometimes faster.

∾∽ Turn.

𝄇   Roll (in drum music).

𝄋 𝄋· 𝄋   Play as if written in eighth notes.

VALUES OF NOTES, RESTS AND DOTS

Name — Notes — Symbol		Name — Rests — Symbol		Values in beats if in 4/4 time.
Double whole	∞ or ‖o‖	Double whole	‖▬‖	8
Whole	o	Whole	▬	4
Half	𝅗𝅥	Half	▬	2
Quarter	𝅘𝅥	Quarter	𝄽	1
Eighth	𝅘𝅥𝅮	Eighth	𝄾	$\frac{1}{2}$
Sixteenth	𝅘𝅥𝅯	Sixteenth	𝄿	$\frac{1}{4}$
Thirty-second	𝅘𝅥𝅰	Thirty-second	𝅀	$\frac{1}{8}$
Sixty-fourth	𝅘𝅥𝅱	Sixty-fourth	𝅁	$\frac{1}{16}$

A dot after a note or rest increases its value by one half.

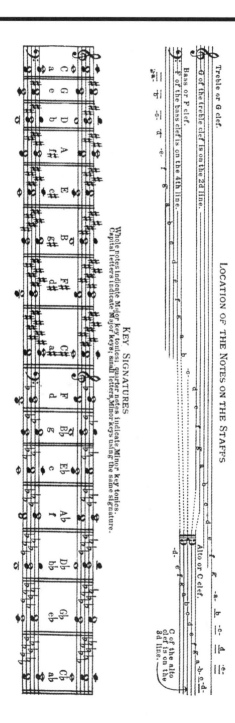

LOCATION OF THE NOTES ON THE STAFFS

Treble or G clef.

G of the treble clef is on the 2d line.

Bass or F clef.

F of the bass clef is on the 4th line.

Alto or C clef.

C of the alto clef is on the 3d line.

KEY SIGNATURES

Whole notes indicate Major key tonics; quarter notes indicate Minor key tonics.
Capital letters indicate Major keys; small letters, Minor keys using the same signature.

INSTRUMENTATION

Arranged For	*May Also Be Used For*
Flutes	Piccolo
Oboes	
1st Bb Clarinet.............. 2nd Bb Clarinet.............. }	Bb Soprano Saxophones
1st Saxophone—Eb Alto...... 2nd Saxophone—Eb Alto...... }	Eb Alto Clarinet Eb Alto Sarrusophone
3rd Saxophone—Bb Tenor.... {	Baritone or Euphonium (treble clef), Bass Clarinet, Bb Tenor Sarrusophone, Bb Bass Sarrusophone or Saxophone, Tenor Horn
4th Saxophone—Eb Baritone.. {	Eb Baritone Sarrusophone
1st Bassoon 2nd Bassoon................	Double Bassoon
1st F Horn................ 2nd F Horn................ {	Basset (Horn, English Horn, F Mellophones
1st Cornet in Bb and A (Solo) 2nd Cornet in Bb and A...... 3rd Cornet in Bb and A...... {	Trumpets, Fluegelhorns, Baritone or Euphonium (treble clef), Bb Soprano Sarrusophone or Saxophone
1st Trombone (*Orchestra*) 2nd Trombone (*Orchestra*)	
Snare Drum, Bass Drum, Timpani, Bells, etc............. {	Includes Cymbals and Triangle. Bell parts may be used for Xylophone, Marimba, Chimes
1st Violin—First position..... (*Amateur or school*) 1st Violin—Higher positions.. (*Professional-solo*) 2nd Violin—Double stops...... (*Professional*)	Mandolin, Steel Guitar, Ocarina Mandolin Mandolin, Tenor Banjo, Ocarinas
2nd Violin—First position..... (*Amateur or school*) 3rd Violin—First position..... (*Amateur or school*) }	Mandolins

⎰Viola—Double stops ....⎱Mandola
⎱ (*Professional*)   ⎰Tenor Banjo
 Viola—First position.........
   (*School*)

⎰'Cello .... Mandocello
⎱Baritone—Bass clef.......... Euphonium

⎰String Bass .... Mandobass
⎱Bass Tuba .... ⎰Helicon Bass, Sousa-
                             ⎱ phone

⎰Db Piccolo
⎱Eb Clarinet

Bb Clarinet—*Solo and Obb.*

⎰1st Eb Horn—Alto...........⎱Eb Mellophones
⎱2nd Eb Horn—Alto...........⎰

⎰1st Trombone (*Band*)
⎱2nd Trombone (*Band*)

⎰1st C Melody Saxophone
⎱2nd C Melody Saxophone